NATIONAL ACADEMIES
Sciences
Engineering
Medicine

NATIONAL
ACADEMIES
PRESS
Washington, DC

I0109539

Examining Prosecution

Convened September 23–24, 2024

Erin Hammers Forstag, *Rapporteur*

Committee on Law and Justice

Division of Behavioral and Social Sciences and Education

Proceedings of a Workshop

NATIONAL ACADEMIES PRESS 500 Fifth Street, NW Washington, DC 20001

This activity was supported by contracts between the National Academy of Sciences and Arnold Ventures (23-09241), the Joyce Foundation (50124), and the William T. Grant Foundation (AWP-000067). Support for the work of the Committee on Law and Justice is provided through the Annie E. Casey Foundation, the National Academy of Sciences W.K. Kellogg Fund, and a grant from the National Institute of Justice (No.15PNIJ-22-GK-00032-NIJB). Any opinions, findings, conclusions, or recommendations expressed in this publication do not necessarily reflect the views of any organization or agency that provided support for the project.

International Standard Book Number-13: 978-0-309- 73435-6
International Standard Book Number-10: 0-309- 73435-5
Digital Object Identifier: https://doi.org/10.17226/29037

This publication is available from the National Academies Press, 500 Fifth Street, NW, Keck 360, Washington, DC 20001; (800) 624-6242; http://www.nap.edu.

Copyright 2025 by the National Academy of Sciences. National Academies of Sciences, Engineering, and Medicine and National Academies Press and the graphical logos for each are all trademarks of the National Academy of Sciences. All rights reserved.

Printed in the United States of America.

Suggested citation: National Academies of Sciences, Engineering, and Medicine. 2025. *Examining Prosecution: Proceedings of a Workshop*. Washington, DC: National Academies Press. https://doi.org/10.17226/29037.

The **National Academy of Sciences** was established in 1863 by an Act of Congress, signed by President Lincoln, as a private, nongovernmental institution to advise the nation on issues related to science and technology. Members are elected by their peers for outstanding contributions to research. Dr. Marcia McNutt is president.

The **National Academy of Engineering** was established in 1964 under the charter of the National Academy of Sciences to bring the practices of engineering to advising the nation. Members are elected by their peers for extraordinary contributions to engineering. Dr. John L. Anderson is president.

The **National Academy of Medicine** (formerly the Institute of Medicine) was established in 1970 under the charter of the National Academy of Sciences to advise the nation on medical and health issues. Members are elected by their peers for distinguished contributions to medicine and health. Dr. Victor J. Dzau is president.

The three Academies work together as the **National Academies of Sciences, Engineering, and Medicine** to provide independent, objective analysis and advice to the nation and conduct other activities to solve complex problems and inform public policy decisions. The National Academies also encourage education and research, recognize outstanding contributions to knowledge, and increase public understanding in matters of science, engineering, and medicine.

Learn more about the National Academies of Sciences, Engineering, and Medicine at **www.nationalacademies.org**.

Consensus Study Reports published by the National Academies of Sciences, Engineering, and Medicine document the evidence-based consensus on the study's statement of task by an authoring committee of experts. Reports typically include findings, conclusions, and recommendations based on information gathered by the committee and the committee's deliberations. Each report has been subjected to a rigorous and independent peer-review process and it represents the position of the National Academies on the statement of task.

Proceedings published by the National Academies of Sciences, Engineering, and Medicine chronicle the presentations and discussions at a workshop, symposium, or other event convened by the National Academies. The statements and opinions contained in proceedings are those of the participants and are not endorsed by other participants, the planning committee, or the National Academies.

Rapid Expert Consultations published by the National Academies of Sciences, Engineering, and Medicine are authored by subject-matter experts on narrowly focused topics that can be supported by a body of evidence. The discussions contained in rapid expert consultations are considered those of the authors and do not contain policy recommendations. Rapid expert consultations are reviewed by the institution before release.

For information about other products and activities of the National Academies, please visit www.nationalacademies.org/about/whatwedo.

PLANNING COMMITTEE ON EXAMINING PROSECUTION

PREETI CHAUHAN (*Chair*), Professor, Psychology Department, John Jay College of Criminal Justice, CUNY
AMANDA AGAN, Associate Professor, Cornell University
MARLENE BIENER, General Counsel, Association of Prosecuting Attorneys
MATTHEW WADE EPPERSON, Associate Professor, Crown Family School of Social Work, Policy, and Practice and Director, Smart Decarceration Project, University of Chicago
BRIAN D. JOHNSON, Professor and Associate Chair of Criminology and Criminal Justice, University of Maryland
BESIKI LUKA KUTATELADZE, Professor, Steven J. Green School of International and Public Affairs, Florida International University

Staff

MAIA JOHNSTONE, Program Officer
SITARA RAHIAB, Senior Program Assistant
STACEY SMIT, Program Coordinator
KAELYN SANDERS, Christine Mirzayan Science and Technology Policy Graduate Fellow (*until May 2024*)
EMILY P. BACKES, Deputy Board Director

Reviewers

This Proceedings of a Workshop was reviewed in draft form by individuals chosen for their diverse perspectives and technical expertise. The purpose of this independent review is to provide candid and critical comments that will assist the National Academies of Sciences, Engineering, and Medicine in making each published proceedings as sound as possible and to ensure that it meets the institutional standards for quality, objectivity, evidence, and responsiveness to the charge. The review comments and draft manuscript remain confidential to protect the integrity of the process.

We thank the following individuals for their review of this proceedings:

AMANDA AGAN, Cornell University
BRIAN D. JOHNSON, University of Maryland

We also thank staff member **BERNA OZTEKIN-GUNAYDIN** for reading and providing helpful comments on this manuscript.

Although the reviewers listed above provided many constructive comments and suggestions, they were not asked to endorse the content of the proceedings nor did they see the final draft before its release. The review of this proceedings was overseen by **ELSA CHEN,** Santa Clara University. She was responsible for making certain that an independent examination of this proceedings was carried out in accordance with standards of the National Academies and that all review comments were carefully considered. Responsibility for the final content rests entirely with the rapporteur and the National Academies.

Acknowledgments

The National Academies of Sciences, Engineering, and Medicine's Committee on Law and Justice (CLAJ) wishes to express its sincere gratitude to the planning committee chair, Preeti Chauhan, for her valuable contributions to the development and orchestration of this workshop. CLAJ also wishes to thank all the members of the planning committee, who collaborated to ensure the workshop included an abundance of informative presentations and moderated discussions. CLAJ would also like to recognize the critical support of the workshop sponsors, Arnold Ventures, the Joyce Foundation, and the William T. Grant Foundation, without which we could not have undertaken this project.

Contents

Box and Figures

BOX

FIGURES

Acronyms and Abbreviations

ADA	assistant district attorney
AI	artificial intelligence
APA	Association of Prosecuting Attorneys
CLAJ	Committee on Law and Justice
DA	district attorney
DOJ	Department of Justice
fi. fa.	fieri facias
FOID	Firearm Owner's Identification
FTA	failure to appear
HBCU	historically Black colleges and universities
JCC	Justice Coordinating Council
JLUSA	JustLeadershipUSA
MCCC	Multi-Cultural Community Center
MFJ	Measures for Justice
MIR	Make it Right
NIJ	National Institute of Justice
PPI	Prosecutorial Performance Indicators
RIPA	racial and identity profiling
UUW	unlawful use of weapon

1

Introduction: Exploring Models of Prosecutorial Programs and Practices

INTRODUCTION

On September 23 and 24, 2024, the Committee on Law and Justice of the National Academies of Sciences, Engineering, and Medicine convened a workshop to explore the practice of prosecution and its impact on incarceration and racial disparities in the criminal justice system. During her opening remarks, Preeti Chauhan, John Jay College of Criminal Justice, CUNY, and workshop planning committee chair, explained that prosecutors increasingly recognize their power, influence, and discretion as possible levers to mitigate racial disparities in the criminal legal system,[1] the growth of incarceration, and incarceration of innocent individuals. Prosecutorial power and discretion are complex matters in a political landscape, said Chauhan. Thus, the goals of the workshop were to highlight practices, programs, and policies that show promise as alternatives to incarceration and that reduce racial and ethnic disparities in criminal justice outcomes; to discuss how prosecutors can improve accountability and their capacity to build community confidence in criminal justice institutions; and to identify data and methodological gaps and opportunities for future research.

---

[1] The terms *criminal legal system* and *criminal justice system* are used interchangeably throughout this workshop proceedings.

BOX 1-1
Statement of Task

The Committee on Law and Justice of the National Academies of Sciences, Engineering, and Medicine will convene a two-day workshop to explore models of prosecutorial programs and practices. The aim of the workshop will be to highlight implications for public policy and priorities for future research.

It will

- Highlight practices, programs, and policies, including gun and violent crime diversion, that show promise as alternatives to incarceration and reducing racial and ethnic disparities in criminal justice outcomes;

- Discuss how prosecutors can improve their capacity to build community confidence in criminal justice institutions, particularly among historically marginalized communities (e.g., by addressing community safety, transparency in decision making, sustainability in reforms);

- Discuss policies, practices, and programs that show promise of building continuous, quality improvement and accountability in prosecutors' offices, particularly those that hold promise for reducing racial and ethnic disparities in criminal justice outcomes and reducing incarceration; and

- Discuss what data and methodological gaps in the research need to be filled in order to address existing gaps in the evidence base.

Chauhan emphasized that, as guided by its statement of task, the workshop aimed to center racial and economic fairness and equity in criminal legal processes and outcomes. Although evidence might not suggest reductions in racial disparities resulting from certain programs or practices, those programs or practices might still be effective in reducing the overall number of individuals negatively impacted by the system, she noted.

Chauhan stressed that prosecution-related research is relatively new compared to research in areas such as policing and incarceration, and that work in this space inherently requires researcher-practitioner partnerships. Prosecutors do not work in isolation, she said, so the workshop featured a diverse array of speakers and perspectives from within the broader criminal legal system and from the community. Chauhan said that the committee attempted to bring in voices from different disciplines, geographies, and perspectives, but she acknowledged that important voices were likely still missing from the room.

ORGANIZATION OF THE WORKSHOP

The workshop, guided by a committee (see Appendix A for committee biosketches) was divided into a series of discussions seeking to address the statement of task (Box 1-1). This proceedings is organized to maximize clarity for a broad audience and do not directly follow the event's agenda order (see Appendix B for workshop agenda). Chapter 2 summarizes discussions on the role of prosecutors in reducing disparities and providing alternatives to criminal justice involvement, and it includes both research findings and promising practices. Chapter 3 examines data use and the data culture within prosecutors' offices. Chapter 4 explores prosecution within the broader criminal justice system, examining the value of collaboration with criminal justice actors and building partnerships with communities. Chapter 5 looks at the future of prosecution; panelists identified future opportunities for research, data, and policy, and reflected on key themes from the workshop.

This proceedings was prepared by the workshop rapporteur as a factual summary of the workshop. The planning committee's role was limited to planning and convening the workshop. The views contained in the proceedings are those of individual workshop participants and do not necessarily represent the views of all workshop participants, the planning committee, or the National Academies of Sciences, Engineering, and Medicine.

2

Research Findings and Promising Practices: Reducing Racial and Ethnic Disparities and Providing Alternatives to Criminal Justice Involvement

Brian D. Johnson, University of Maryland and workshop planning committee member, and Preeti Chauhan moderated sessions on the role of prosecutors in reducing disparities and providing alternatives to the criminal justice system. Discussions address factors that shape prosecutors' decisions, ways prosecutors' decisions intentionally alleviate or unintentionally exacerbate existing inequalities in the criminal legal system, and practices for implementing alternative approaches to incarceration without sacrificing public safety. Until recently, said Johnson, little information was available to answer these questions—prosecutorial decision making was a "black box" that was seldom examined in research and little understood outside the prosecutor community.

However, a noticeable shift has occurred in the past 20 years, said Johnson, in part due to historical factors (e.g., increasing incarceration in the United States in the 1980s and 1990s) that resulted in growing scrutiny of sentencing and correctional policies. Declining crime rates beginning in the early 1990s raised questions about the laws and practices that lead to those high incarceration rates. Despite recent decarceration efforts, said Johnson, the United States continues to have historically high imprisonment rates, with the burden of incarceration disproportionately borne by African American, Hispanic, and American Indian individuals (National Academies of Sciences, Engineering, and Medicine, 2023). Increasingly, academics, practitioners, policymakers, and the public have begun calling for new approaches to address racial inequalities and to reduce the footprint of criminal justice involvement in America, said Johnson. Historically, these efforts have tended to focus narrowly on judges and their sentencing choices, but the focus has shifted as people have recognized the power of prosecutors to shape criminal justice outcomes. Quoting Wesley Bell, a former prosecutor in St. Louis County,

Johnson said that prosecutors can fill prisons, destroy lives, and exacerbate racial disparities, but they also have the power to do the opposite.

Over the past two decades, research efforts have significantly advanced the understanding of factors that shape prosecutors' decision making, said Johnson. He highlighted three findings from this work. First, research findings remain mixed regarding racial and ethnic disparities, and many studies reveal that Black and Latino defendants do not necessarily receive the most punitive outcomes, despite conventional wisdom. In fact, he said, some research demonstrated that, under certain circumstances, prosecutors are exercising their discretion in ways that directly address racial injustice (e.g., Mitchell et al., 2022; Mitchell & Petersen, 2024; Shaffer, 2023).

Second, Johnson noted a nascent evidence base suggesting that racial disparities often emerge in alternatives to incarceration and other discretionary decisions related to diversion (e.g., Engen et al., 2003; Johnson & DiPietro, 2012; Nicosia et al., 2017). These disparities could be due to a lack of structure in the mechanisms used to identify diversion candidates or could be tied to other structural criteria that unintentionally disadvantage certain types of defendants, he suggested. Such criteria might include requirements related to criminal history records or requirements for defendants to pay for alternatives to incarceration. However, said Johnson, prosecutors' offices are increasingly identifying and offering redress for inequities in such decisions.

The third research finding of note regards the cumulative and interacting nature of decision making in the criminal legal system. Johnson noted a growing consensus that prosecutors and other court actors make consequential decisions daily and that those decisions are inherently related to one another (e.g., Johnson et al., 2016; Kurlycheck & Johnson, 2019; Kutateladze et al., 2014). For example, recent work suggests that offices with a higher proportion of cases screened out at initial charging tend to have fewer case dismissals later in the process (Prosecutorial Performance Indicators, 2022). This suggests that a broad lens is required to examine the manifold complementary decisions that collectively shape case outcomes, said Johnson, as well as to fully grasp how prosecutorial discretion can be exercised to help address overarching inequality in the criminal legal system.

The goal of the first workshop sessions, noted Johnson, was to examine the evidence regarding the use of data-driven and evidence-based approaches in several areas: to address existing inequalities, to implement and test innovative policy solutions aimed at increasing diversion alternatives, and to improve long-term outcomes for defendants. He noted a need to improve data transparency and accountability in prosecution, provide victims and community members with a meaningful voice in the process, and continue building community confidence in and perceptions of procedural justice in prosecution, all while working to reduce the footprint of incarceration without sacrificing public safety.

These goals are emerging across social and political contexts throughout the country and in prosecutors' offices of varying sizes, said Johnson, driven by a growing appreciation and concern for the disproportionate impact of unintended criminal justice-related harms on certain racial and socioeconomic groups. Despite ongoing research challenges, he estimated that, over the last 25 years, more progress has been made in the study of prosecution than in any other domain of the criminal legal system. A growing number of large-scale, detailed data-collection efforts exist across diverse offices and geographic locales, conducted by a broad group of scholars including economists, political scientists, criminologists, legal scholars, and nonprofit research organizations. Efforts to evaluate data-driven policy changes and improve transparency and accountability have been aided by growth in research-practitioner partnerships, including those between prosecutors' offices and academic research partners. Such partnerships employ innovations like public-facing dashboards, community town hall meetings, and self-published reports on racial and ethnic justice, Johnson said.

Despite the expansion in quasiexperimental and causal research on the effects of prosecutorial decision making, as well as in the number of rigorous evaluations of the effects of specific prosecutorial policies in various jurisdictions, said Johnson, several research and policy challenges remain. The overall evidence base for best practices in prosecution and policy recommendations remains underdeveloped, he noted. These workshop sessions represent an important step in identifying what is known, what remains to be learned, and what policies and practices appear to be most promising for reducing racial and ethnic disparities and encouraging alternatives to incarceration, he said.

Johnson and Chauhan moderated sessions (see Appendix B) during which speakers discussed the impact of prosecutorial decision points. Presentations covered topics including the salutary effects that declining to prosecute can have on racial disparities, results from diversion programs, the effectivity of prosecutorial charging decisions in offsetting inequalities from earlier stages of the criminal justice pipeline, and the potential association of racial disparities with various outcomes, such as declinations, transfer, and diversion decisions.

EMPIRICAL EVIDENCE ON PROSECUTION

Evidence on Case Declination

The first decision point for prosecutors, said Amanda Agan, Cornell University, is the decision whether to charge or decline to prosecute a case. This is a crucial initial step in the adjudication process in terms of both public safety and recidivism, she noted. The choice to prosecute or not to prosecute can be met with backlash from community members, police, and politicians with different perspectives, said Agan. From one perspective, defendants who are caught and punished for minor crimes may be less likely to commit future crimes. On the other hand, criminal records can have myriad consequences that may increase future offenses, including impacts on housing, employment, and access to public services. Within this context, Agan and her colleagues collaborated with a prosecutor's office to analyze data from Suffolk County, Massachusetts (Boston) case management files. Comparing outcomes for prosecuted and nonprosecuted defendants showed that those who were not prosecuted were less likely to have another criminal complaint over the next two years.

However, said Agan, this decreased likelihood could be due to either the choice to not prosecute or to differences between cases that are prosecuted and those that are not prosecuted. For instance, explained Agan, individuals who are not prosecuted are more likely to be citizens, less likely to have a conviction in the previous year, and the crimes are more likely to be victimless and not involve disorder or theft. The different "styles" of prosecuted and unprosecuted cases, said Agan, makes the relationship between nonprosecution and a lower likelihood of recidivism difficult to understand. The practices of the Suffolk County court system presented an opportunity for research into this relationship.

Suffolk County assigns nonviolent misdemeanor complaints to arraignment courtrooms without regard to the identity of the arraigning Assistant District Attorney (ADA) or defendant, explained Agan. During the research sample period of 2004–2018, 315 ADAs rotated in and out of hearing arraignments. These ADAs varied in their rates of declining cases at arraignment, she said, with declination rates ranging from 10 percent to 50 percent and an average of 20.5 percent.

The mix of case characteristics was similar between low-leniency and high-leniency ADAs (as if randomly assigned), she explained, but the decisions the ADAs made were different. For cases with particularly strong or weak evidence, the assigned ADA may not have mattered, said Agan; these defendants were likely to be prosecuted (or not) regardless of which ADA made the decision. However, for many defendants, the random assignment of the ADA impacted whether the case was prosecuted. This natural experiment allowed researchers to examine these defendants and estimate the impact of the decision to prosecute (Agan et al., 2023).

Researchers looked at the two-year period after a decision to prosecute or not prosecute, and found that, for cases in which the assignment of the ADA mattered for the arraignment outcome, the decision to not prosecute a nonviolent misdemeanor case was associated with the following:

- A 58-percent decrease in the probability of a new criminal complaint;
- A 69-percent decrease in the number of new criminal complaints;
- A 67-percent decrease in the number of new misdemeanor complaints; and
- A 75-percent decrease in the number of new felony complaints.

These results, said Agan, were concentrated among first-time defendants who did not have measurable previous criminal legal contact in Suffolk County. This finding suggests that, for defendants with previous criminal records, additional leniency does not significantly decrease recidivism. Thus, the collateral consequences of criminal legal contact may be partially driving the recidivism effect. Defendants who can avoid the mark of a criminal record have decreased recidivism, but once defendants are "marked," further leniency does not continue to reduce recidivism, she stated.

Limitations and Future Research Needed on Declination

Agan noted that these findings are based only on research from one county over one 14-year period. She and her colleagues are working with New York County, New York, to replicate and extend the research; further, similar research in other jurisdictions, including smaller towns and additional areas of the country, is warranted, she said. Additionally, this research focused only on cases of nonviolent misdemeanors, but further research could explore cases of violent misdemeanors or felonies. Another limitation, said Agan, involved insufficient data on race and ethnicity, complicating the detection of outcome differences based on those characteristics. Finally, she said, the study only examined the impact of prosecutorial decisions on recidivism. Recidivism might be the easiest thing to measure, Agan emphasized, but it is not the only important outcome. Studying other outcomes, such as impacts on employment, housing, and well-being, would require linking data across agencies. While often difficult, this type of cross-agency collaboration is necessary to gain a full understanding of the consequences of prosecutorial decisions and practices, Agan said.

In response to a workshop participant's question, Agan noted the difficulty of studying the impact of a declination policy on actual crime rates due to reporting and police referral issues. For example, police and the public may change their behavior in response to the lack of prosecution of certain crimes—for example, the public may not report such crimes, and the police may not bring those crimes to the prosecutor. On the other hand, she said, the opposite could occur—in attempt to demonstrate that nonviolent misdemeanors are a problem in the community, the public or the police could increasingly report or refer those crimes. Examine the impact of a declination policy on crime would necessitate a broader measure of crime that is not related to reporting, said Agan. For example, researchers could use data on retail shrinkage rates (i.e., loss of retail inventory), or 911 call information that is not brought to the prosecutor. Further research is warranted in this area, she said.

Evidence from Diversion Programs

Speakers provided an overview of diversion programs, including promising practices and research gaps. To set the stage for speaker presentations, Matthew Epperson, The University of Chicago and workshop planning committee member, briefly outlined the history and purpose of diversion programs.

Prosecutors face a variety of urgent issues that impact safety and justice in their jurisdictions, said Epperson. Considering the growing national interest in reducing incarceration and addressing racial disparities, prosecutors have a critical role to play. Many jurisdictions are grappling with an overwhelming number of lower-level or low-priority cases, and prosecutors are often tasked with balancing resources with case priority. Together, these circumstances have led many prosecutors to reenvision their roles in the criminal legal system and to rethink the definition of successful prosecutorial outcomes, said Epperson. He noted the range of possible outcomes for a case, from dismissal to conviction, with diversion as one outcome within this range. Diversion programs were first developed in the 1930s for juveniles and began to be used in the adult system in the 1970s. The use of diversion programs has expanded over the last 10–15 years, he said.

Diversion programs can be thought of as a programmatic encapsulation of prosecutorial discretion, Epperson said. A prosecutor may exercise their discretion to divert certain classes of cases or certain types of defendants. When a defendant enters a diversion program, prosecution is put on hold, and successful completion of the program results in dismissal of charges. Program requirements range from minimal and short term to intensive and long term. Diversion can also be framed as a two-pronged approach, Epperson said. The first prong is removing the traditional prosecution process, along with the associated collateral consequences. The second prong is replacing prosecution with services that are more likely to meet the defendant's needs. Diversion is a more varied and nuanced approach, he said, compared to the "blunt instrument of prosecution, conviction, and punishment." Diversion also presents an opportunity for prosecutors' offices to reduce the volume and cost of cases, allowing greater focus on higher-priority cases.

Evidence on diversion is promising but mixed, said Epperson. Many new programs only have evidence available for process outcomes like program completion. Prosecutor-led diversion programs tend to have high completion rates, often between 70–90 percent. Most research shows promising outcomes for those who complete the programs, although limitations exist in terms of appropriate comparison groups and study design rigor, he said (e.g., Cossyleon et al., 2017; Epperson et al., 2023; Rempel et al., 2018).

Research Findings: Diversion for Nonviolent Charges

Michael Rempel, Data Collaborative for Justice, explained that diversion programs began to expand in the 1990s, with a high growth mark for "problem-solving courts"—courts focused on one type of offense or type of person (e.g., drug courts or domestic violence courts)—in the early 2000s. Models of diversion programs include police-led, prosecutor-led, and court-led problem-solving courts (i.e., in which prosecutors serve as gatekeepers), explained Rempel. Over half (55%) of prosecutors have reported engaging in prosecutor-led diversion. A multisite evaluation of prosecutor-led diversion programs, funded by the National Institute of Justice

(NIJ), gathered data on 16 programs and evaluated the impact and cost of a subset of these programs (Rempel et al., 2018). Many participating prosecutors' offices were in large jurisdictions where many individuals could potentially be diverted. The programs used a variety of models, Rempel said, including prefiling diversion, postfiling diversion, and mixed models. Unlike early diversion programs, which focused almost exclusively on people facing first-time misdemeanor charges, most of these programs allowed eligibility for people with prior convictions (14 programs) and/or felonies (9 programs). The programs largely did not use evidence-based practices or individualized treatments, said Rempel, relying instead on educational classes, community service, or therapy. One program in Milwaukee, however, utilized a structured risk assessment and tailored the intervention accordingly.[2]

Researchers examined the impact of six diversion programs on recidivism rates, said Rempel, and found reductions in rearrest in five programs, three of which were statistically significant. These results were unexpected—researchers anticipated a null effect because the programs were either too short to have an impact or used methods (e.g., education) that have not been proven effective. Why, Rempel asked, did these programs impact recidivism? He offered several potential answers based on focus groups with participants. First, participants felt a greater sense of procedural justice—that is, they felt they received compassion and fair treatment. Second, participants had a perceived sense of substantive justice; they appreciated the case dismissal and the avoidance of a criminal record. Third, participants did not suffer collateral harm from a conviction (e.g., stigma, socioeconomic harm, and psychological harm), which may have contributed to program impact. This suggests, said Rempel, that choosing not to prosecute could have the same impact on recidivism as a diversion program; that is, "doing nothing works." State's Attorney Kimberly Foxx, Cook County, Illinois, added that "doing nothing" may impact other parts of the system. For example, when Foxx chose to forego drug diversion programs and instead drop drug charges for those at low risk of reoffense, drug cases dropped significantly. She explained that law enforcement had no incentive to make the arrest in the first place since they knew prosecutors would not take the cases. While dropping the charges alarmed some people, she said, the alternative diversion programs were "performative" and not proven effective.

---

[2] For more information, see Rempel et al., 2018, p. 18.

The NIJ-funded multistate study had some limitations, said Rempel—namely, the diversion programs largely did not use evidence-based practices, and nearly all excluded people facing violent charges. More research is warranted to determine which practices work, and whether these models are applicable to people charged with violence, he noted. Further, most diversion programs are measured against traditional prosecution rather than the "nothing counterfactual" (i.e., not prosecuting), which makes isolating the program's impact difficult. Many included programs were small, said Rempel, resulting in a small sample size and limited impact on over-incarceration.

Research Findings: Effectiveness of Diversion in San Francisco

San Francisco has a robust set of postfiling, pretrial diversion programs, said Steven Raphael, University of California (UC), Berkley, and a long history of experimenting with reform. A research partnership between the San Francisco District Attorney's (DA) Office and the California Policy Lab at UC Berkeley generated several studies over the past decade, including decision-point analysis of race disparities in criminal case processing, disparate impacts of California reforms on case dispositions by race, descriptive studies of existing diversion programs, causal analysis of adult diversion for felony cases, and a randomized controlled trial evaluation of a youth restorative justice program. Raphael highlighted two studies for discussion: one on the impact of felony diversion (Augustine et al., 2022), and another on the impact of a restorative justice program on recidivism (Shem-Tov et al., 2024).

For individuals served with felonies, San Francisco's potential avenues for diversion include behavioral health court, drug court, veterans court, and young adult court. If an individual completes a diversion program, charges are generally dropped, Raphael said. People referred to diversion in San Francisco tend to have a long history of criminal involvement, he said, with high risk of recidivism. Some San Francisco judges use diversion programs heavily, while others are less likely to do so. As cases are randomly assigned to judges, studying the impact of diversion on outcomes is possible. Researchers examined approximately 17,000 felony cases that were eligible for diversion, with arrests between 2009–2017. One of the main differences identified, said Raphael, was that individuals in a diversion program spent far more time in the criminal justice system; diverted cases took about 250 days longer to be disposed than traditional cases did. Raphael explained that diversion programs involve "heavy intervention," including the provision of services and frequent check-ins. San Francisco prosecutors told researchers that they reserve diversion programs for individuals with serious criminal backgrounds; in general, first-time offenders with low-level felonies would not be offered diversion.

Researchers examined the impact of diversion on outcomes over two-year (Figure 2-1) and five-year (Figure 2-2) periods. Patterns were similar in both analyses, said Raphael, with individuals who completed diversion being somewhat less likely to be rearrested and even less likely to be reconvicted than those who received traditional adjudication. These results demonstrate that diversion appears to be more effective at reducing recidivism than traditional case adjudication.

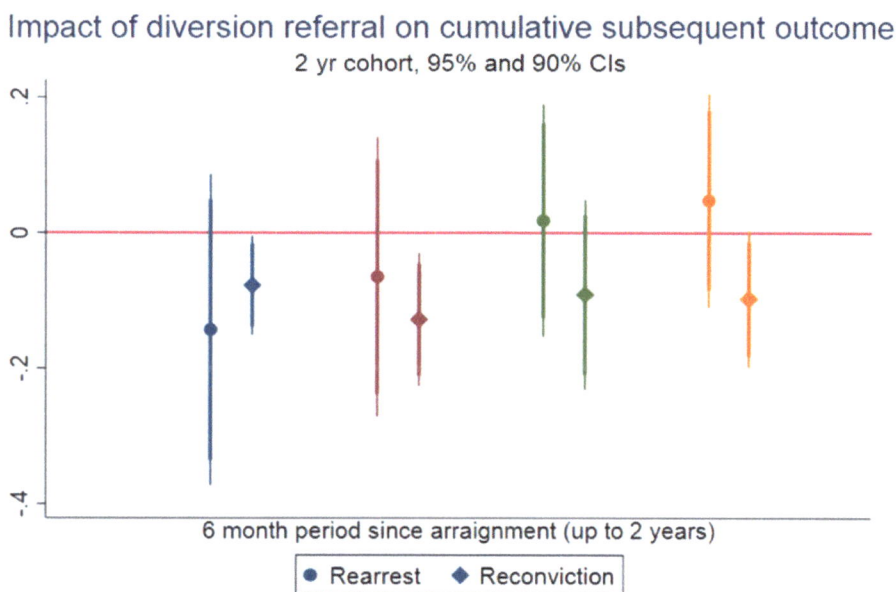

FIGURE 2-1 Impact of diversion referral on cumulative subsequent outcome, two years.
NOTE: Pairs of bars along the x-axis represent increasing six-month intervals (i.e., 6 months, 12 months, 18 months, 24 months). In the figure title, "CIs" refer to confidence intervals.
SOURCE: Augustine et al., 2022; presented by Steven Raphael on September 23, 2024.

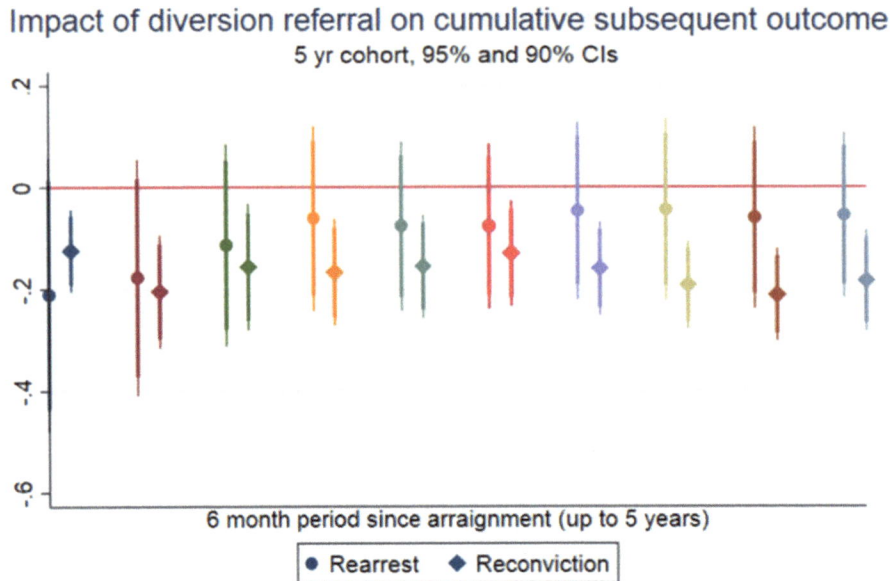

FIGURE 2-2 Impact of diversion referral on cumulative subsequent outcome, five years.
NOTE: Pairs of bars along the x-axis represent increasing six-month intervals (i.e., 6 months, 12 months, 18 months, etc.). In the figure title, "CIs" refer to confidence intervals.
SOURCE: Augustine et al., 2022; presented by Steven Raphael on September 23, 2024.

Next, Raphael discussed a second study examining the impact of a restorative justice program on recidivism. Make It Right (MIR) is a San Francisco youth restorative justice program that serves as an alternative to criminal prosecution. Youth arrested for a felony are eligible for the program if they are not affiliated with a gang, are not on probation or in detention at time of arrest, did not injure the victim or use a weapon, and have no prior offenses that count as a strike under California's Three Strikes and You're Out law.[3] The program was studied using a randomized controlled trial from 2013–2019; with the victims' consent, the trial randomized eligible youth to one of two groups: prosecution as usual or participation in MIR. Community Works West[4] implemented the MIR program by facilitating a restorative justice conference between the victim and the implicated youth. The conference resulted in an agreement between victim and offender, with the goal of restoring the victim's welfare. This could include repainting the victim's graffitied garage or agreeing to attend school regularly, said Raphael. Another

---

[3] For more information, see
https://leginfo.legislature.ca.gov/faces/codes_displaySection.xhtml?lawCode=PEN&sectionNum=667
[4] For more information, see https://communityworkswest.org/

group, Huckleberry Youth Center, managed the postconference case management and compliance monitoring. If the youth did not follow through on the agreement, said Raphael, he or she was sent back to the DA for prosecution. Law enforcement received no information about the program and was not involved, other than to dismiss charges if the youth successfully completed the program or to refile charges if not.

Of the 44 youth randomly assigned to traditional criminal prosecution, 43.2 percent were rearrested within 6 months and 56.8 percent were rearrested within 12 months. Of the 80 youth randomly assigned to MIR and found to be suitable for the program, 52 completed it and 26 did not. Rearrest numbers for those who did not complete MIR were similar to numbers for those who underwent traditional prosecution, with 34.6 percent rearrested within 6 months and 57.7 percent within 12 months. However, youth who completed MIR had significantly lower rearrest rates—only 11.5 percent were rearrested within 6 months and 19.2 percent within 12 months. Further, said Raphael, data showed that MIR was associated with a permanent reduction in rearrests, with arrest rates around 24 percentage points lower up to four years later.

Raphael cautioned that, while results are promising, the trial was small. He noted that the ADA in charge of youth filings was "very hesitant" about the program at the beginning and greatly restricted who could participate. However, by the end of the study, the ADA expressed their belief in the value of the MIR program.

Research Findings: Pathway to New Beginnings Program

Epperson described research conducted specifically on diversion programs for gun-related charges. In 2021, Epperson and his colleagues surveyed the country for gun diversion programs and found eight programs, nearly all of which were targeted at illegal gun possession (Sharif-Kazemi et al., 2021). The programs used a variety of approaches, including restorative justice, therapy, resource provision, and anger management and life skills training. Epperson and colleagues asked prosecutors about their motivations for using diversion programs. One reported motivation was a concern about racial disparities. Epperson noted that prosecutors are constantly navigating and balancing constituents' public safety concerns with the high level of racial disparities in gun-related cases. Black men constitute an overwhelming proportion of individuals arrested with gun possession charges, said Epperson. Young Black men are "over-surveilled and over-policed," and often have safety concerns that increase their likelihood of carrying a gun. Together, he said, these factors contribute to increased contact with the criminal justice system.

Another motivation for prosecutors, said Epperson, was the ineffectiveness of traditional prosecution and incarceration in gun possession cases for preventing gun violence. When prosecutors examined their data, said Epperson, they found that when people charged with low-level offenses were prosecuted to the fullest extent, many ended up returning to the system with escalated gun-related charges. Universal prosecution and incarceration may not be the appropriate response to every case, Epperson said; prosecutors are beginning to recognize this and pursue alternatives. Prosecutors using diversion also reported being motivated by the ability to differentiate between types of gun charges. Gun possession does not necessarily translate to gun violence, said Epperson, and diverting possession cases may enable prosecutors to focus on more serious cases.

A Minneapolis prosecutor-led diversion program called Pathway to New Beginnings was established in 2017. Eligible individuals were those with a gross misdemeanor weapons offense, no prior felony convictions or gun/violence convictions, and were not currently on probation. Minneapolis City Attorney Susan Segal observed that many individuals arrested for gross misdemeanor weapons offenses were young adults with various levels of structural and individual disadvantage, noted Epperson. Since prosecuting and convicting these individuals improved neither their trajectory nor community safety, the diversion program was created as an alternative. The program consisted of two phases starting with a 12-week intensive phase of therapy, mentoring, and ongoing case management. The second phase, lasting two to six months, had less intensive programming and was followed by a year of probation with no programming. Individuals were terminated from the program if they failed to complete requirements or if they received a new charge related to guns or violence. Researchers examined recidivism rates for both successful and unsuccessful participants, along with a comparison group with similar characteristics (Figure 2-3) (Epperson et al., 2024). Of the 76 program participants, 53 (69.7%) successfully completed the program, and 23 (30%) were terminated due to loss of contact or engagement, a new charge, or other circumstances. Two years after the initial weapons charge, 51.6 percent of the comparison group had a charge involving a weapon or interpersonal violence, and 40.9 percent had a conviction. Of the participants who successfully completed the program, 26.4 percent had a charge, and 13.2 percent had a conviction. Epperson noted that the higher rates of charges and convictions for the failed program participants were unsurprising given that many failed participants were terminated due to a new charge.

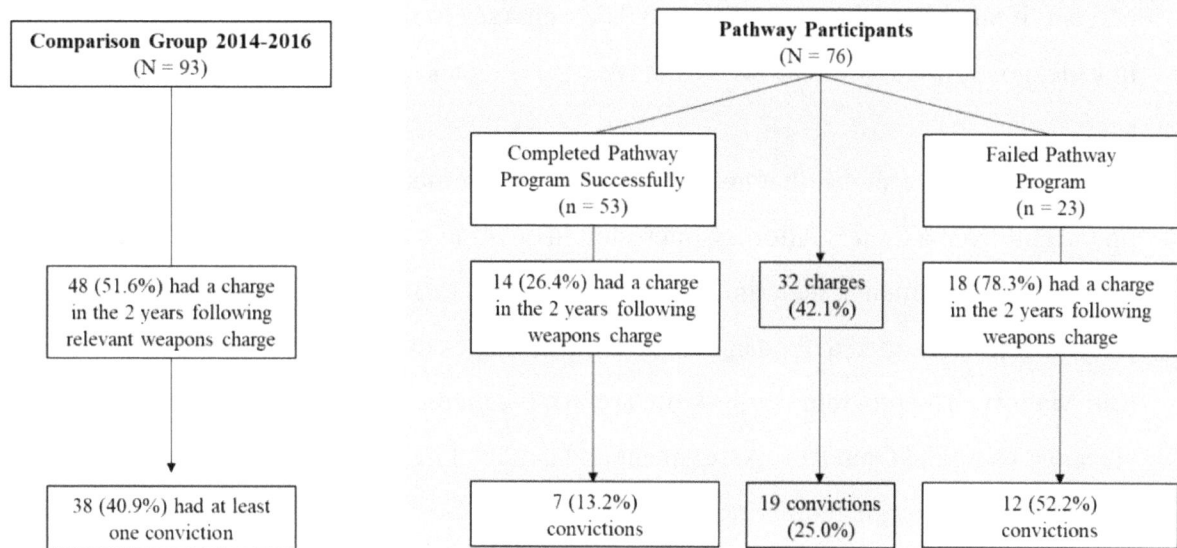

FIGURE 2-3 Pathway to New Beginnings outcomes.
SOURCE: Epperson et al., 2024; presentation by Matthew Epperson on September 23, 2024.

Diversion program graduates had significantly lower odds of arrest, conviction, and weapon/violence arrest within two years of the initial charge, said Epperson. These data suggest that a diversion program can be implemented without jeopardizing public safety, and that these programs may hold promise for reducing racial disparities. The program's high graduation rate indicates its feasibility as an intervention, he said. Further research on gun diversion programs is currently underway, and programs are expanding eligibility to reach more potential participants. Areas for continued research, said Epperson, include measuring outcomes beyond recidivism, studying the impact of expungement, and examining the participant experience.

Promising Practice: GRO Community

God.Restoring.Order (GRO) Community is a community mental health center located on the far south side of Chicago, specializing in clinical services for boys and men—particularly boys and men of color, said Aaron Mallory, GRO Community.[5] The organization launched a gun diversion program in 2022. Mallory outlined the program and the people it serves. Nationally, said Mallory, firearm offenders have a higher rate of recidivism (68%) than nonfirearm offenders

[5] For more information see https://grocommunity.org/

(46.3%). Most people arrested for firearm offenses are African American men, who represent 74 percent of all unlawful use of weapon (UUW) charges in Illinois. Furthermore, 11 communities in Chicago—primarily on the south and west sides—make up one-third of the UUW cases in the state.

Mallory explained that his presentations at community forums on mental health led to a phone call from a State's Attorney interested in creating a diversion program to address the large number of Black men in the criminal justice system. The two created a six-month gun diversion program that permitted defendants to have their charges dropped upon successful completion, said Mallory. The program begins with a referral from the State's Attorney; individuals are then screened using the Ohio Risk Assessment and a mental health assessment. Program staff talk about expectations and requirements, and individuals are assigned a group counselor and an individual counselor. A graduation ceremony is held for individuals who complete the program. The intervention's intensity varies depending on the individual's risk level for recidivism. For example, individuals at low risk participate in group counseling twice a week and individual counseling every other week, while individuals at moderate-high risk have group counseling three times a week and weekly individual counseling. Group counseling began virtually because of the COVID-19 pandemic, said Mallory, and the virtual format worked well. The program also involves cognitive behavioral interventions, using a the Choose 24:7 Cognitive Behavioral Therapy curriculum. This curriculum, developed by GRO Community, helps people identify situations in which they feel they need a firearm, work on their thoughts within these settings, and develop ways to minimize or navigate those risky situations. The intervention uses role playing and group activities, said Mallory, and GRO Community is currently working to develop a virtual reality version of the program.

The first cohort of the gun diversion program had 73 participants, 71 of whom were African American, with a mean age of 27. Nearly all had high school diplomas (93%), many had some college (42%), and almost half (49%) were employed at the time of arrest. In Chicago, Mallory explained, there is a prevailing belief that people arrested for illegal gun possession are "bad people" who are involved in gangs or drugs. Through this program, he said, it became clear that most of these men were "individuals who are just trying to take care of their families." The risk-need-responsivity assessment, which identifies factors that lead to recidivism, determined that a majority of participants were low risk for recidivism. As the program continued, said

Mallory, the State's Attorney's office began referring higher-risk individuals. Overall, 47 participants were low risk for recidivism, 20 at moderate risk, and 4 at high risk. Of the 73 participants, 63 completed the program and 10 did not complete it due to noncompliance or another charge.

As part of the diversion program, said Mallory, GRO Community conducted qualitative research to identify reasons why participants felt the need to carry a gun. Three main themes emerged: protection, legal cynicism, and permissibility of concealed carry in Illinois. One participant said that he had been shot before and did not want it to happen again; another participant said that he had previously been robbed at gunpoint and the police refused to respond. This feeling of legal cynicism was pervasive, said Mallory, with many participants expressing their belief that police would not protect them. Finally, some participants did not understand concealed carry laws and thought they could carry a gun as long as they could produce their Firearm Owner's Identification (FOID) card. In fact, said Mallory, 63 percent of participants had a FOID card at the time of arrest.

In 2023, Illinois passed legislation to amend the Unified Code of Corrections,[6] to make the First Time Weapons Offender Program permanent and change some of its eligibility criteria. The diversion program allows individuals over 21 facing charges for the first time to receive probation of 18–24 months instead of a prison sentence. This changed the gun diversion program, said Mallory, because the intrinsic motivation for individuals to participate has lessened. Defense attorneys may steer their clients away from the diversion program because it is more intensive than probation. Despite this challenge, GRO Community is expanding the gun diversion program into new jurisdictions, including other counties with different demographics. They are also increasing enrollment of individuals at moderate and high risk of recidivism. These expansions will allow GRO Community to collect more data on participants and understand which types of interventions work and how to best support participants. Research strategies may include a quasiexperimental design, a randomized controlled trial, qualitative analysis, and latent curve modeling.

---

[6] For more information, see Illinois Senate Bill 0424: https://www.ilga.gov/legislation/billstatus.asp?DocNum=0424&GAID=17&GA=103&DocTypeID=SB&LegID=144172&SessionID=112

EVIDENCE ON RACIAL AND ETHNIC DISPARITIES THROUGHOUT THE PROSECUTION PROCESS

Research Findings: Examining Disparities Using Case Processing Records from Florida

Racial and ethnic disparities may be created, increased, or decreased at each key decision point in the criminal justice process from arrest to final disposition, said Ojmarrh Mitchell, University of California, Irvine. Mitchell described research he and his colleagues conducted to examine potential disparities at some of these decision points (Mitchell et al., 2022). First, Mitchell described a Florida-based study using the state's Sunshine Laws—regulations requiring certain government information be publicly available—to gain access to information on case processing and outcomes. Researchers identified a random sample of felonies filed in each county in 2017, coded the court records to document outcomes, and linked criminal history information to the defendants. Florida's system for case processing, explained Mitchell, has three substantive stages: complaint, information, and adjudication. At the complaint stage, initial charges are filed, and bail is determined. At the information stage, the prosecutor decides whether to file charges as a felony, reduce to a misdemeanor, divert from prosecution, or dismiss the case. At adjudication, a plea agreement specifies the type and length of sanction, which are heavily influenced by negotiations with prosecutors, Mitchell said. Adjudication can be withheld for "uncoerced plea bargain," meaning that a person is found guilty, but the sentence is not enacted. Cases generally result in one of seven outcomes, said Mitchell: case dismissal, transfer to a lower court, diversion from prosecution, withholding of adjudication, probation, jail, or prison. The features of this process give prosecutors great influence over case processing and sentencing outcomes, he said.

Mitchell and his colleagues analyzed the predicted probabilities of each case outcome, by race of the defendant, after controlling for defendant and case characteristics. In the Florida cases, regardless of defendants' race and ethnicity, approximately 25 percent of cases resulted in dismissal and approximately 45 percent were either dismissed, transferred, or diverted. Comparison of Hispanic and White defendants, said Mitchell, revealed few meaningful differences. However, comparison of Black and White defendants showed few differences in the early stages, but racial disparities emerged during the sentencing phase (Figure 2-4).

Specifically, he said, Black defendants were more likely to be sentenced to prison and less likely to receive probation sentences.

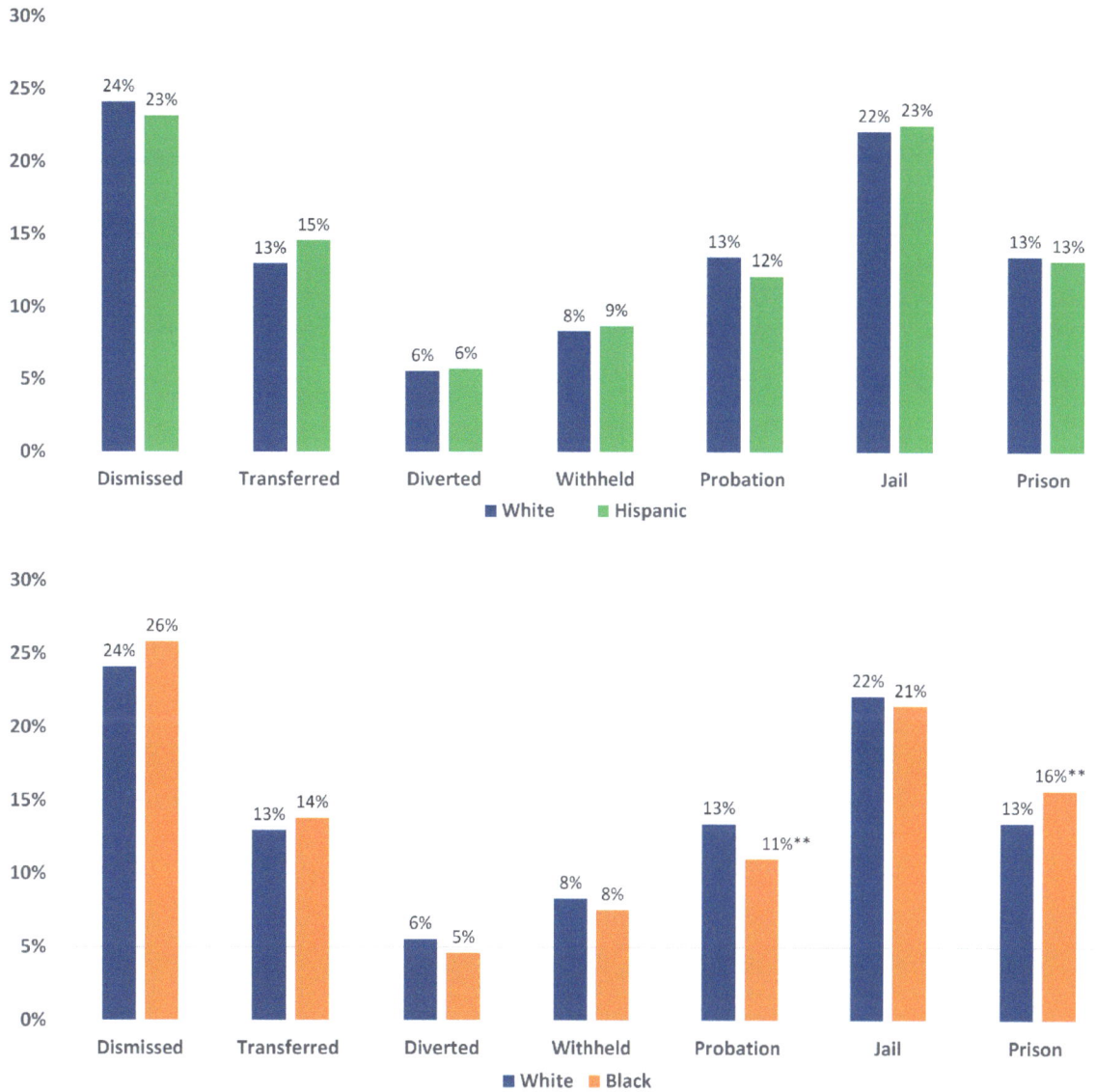

FIGURE 2-4 Case outcomes by race and ethnicity.
SOURCE: Presentation by Ojmarrh Mitchell, September 23, 2024.

Findings describing no Hispanic disadvantage at any stage but a Black disadvantage during sentencing are similar to findings of a systematic review conducted by Mitchell and colleagues (Spohn et al., 2024a; 2024b). The review found that, in state courts, there is a small-to-modest racial/ethnic disadvantage in case filing and case dismissal, some racial/ethnic disadvantage in charge reductions, and Black disadvantage in sentencing outcomes. Notably, said Mitchell, studies examining full case processing are rare.

Mitchell and colleagues examined the public statements and campaign promises of the elected chief prosecutors in each of Florida's 20 judicial circuits (Mitchell et al., 2022). The researchers classified prosecutors as "progressive" if they met three of four criteria: (1) use of "smart"/data-driven decision making, (2) implementation of a conviction integrity unit, (3) a policy to categorically decline/divert certain low-level offenses, and (4) an express commitment to remove "poverty traps," such as cash bail or nonfinancial driver's license reinstatement. Based on these criteria, four chief prosecutors were deemed "progressive" and the remaining sixteen were classified as "conventional," said Mitchell.

Comparison of progressive and conventional prosecutors found that cases adjudicated under progressive prosecutors were more likely to be dismissed, transferred, or diverted. The differences for each outcome were not statistically significant on their own, Mitchell explained, but taken together, the probability of not receiving a felony conviction was approximately 50 percent for progressive prosecutors and 40 percent for conventional prosecutors. This finding was only possible because the researchers examined the full set of case outcomes, Mitchell noted; this is an important approach to studying racial disparities and court outcomes, he stated.

Next, researchers examined whether racial and ethnic disparities at each stage differed under progressive and conventional prosecutors. They found few differences between White and Hispanic defendants, regardless of whether the prosecutor was progressive or conventional, said Mitchell. However, for Black defendants, outcomes varied significantly depending on prosecutor type. Under progressive prosecutors, there were more case dismissals for Black defendants than White, there was no disparity in prison sentences, and the disparity in probation sentences was halved. Cases adjudicated in jurisdictions headed by progressive prosecutors were more likely to be resolved in a manner that did not lead to felony conviction. These findings, said Mitchell, suggest that conventional chief prosecutors and their offices are responsible for the overall disparities that disadvantage Black defendants in case outcomes in Florida.

Research Findings: Impact of Prosecutorial Discretion on Racial Disparities

Racial disparities in incarceration have decreased over the last two decades, said Hannah Shaffer, Harvard Law School, but disparities still exist. Disparities in incarceration can be measured by examining the ratio between the share of Black Americans who are incarcerated and the share of non-Black Americans who are incarcerated, Shaffer explained. In 2005, she said, Black Americans nationwide were almost six times more likely to be incarcerated; by 2020, this had decreased to just under four times more likely. The numbers and trends are similar in North Carolina, where Shaffer has conducted research (Shaffer, 2023).

Several possible reasons exist for the decline in disparities over time, said Shaffer. For example, police are changing their behavior and becoming less likely to arrest Black Americans relative to non-Black Americans. However, she said, while racial disparities in arrests have declined, incarceration disparities have declined more. Another possibility involves changes in the postarrest system, including changes to prosecutorial discretion. Isolating the role of discretion in the court system is difficult, said Shaffer, because case outcomes reflect more than just discretionary decisions. For instance, a prosecutor may be forced to reduce a defendant's charge due to insufficient evidence.

To isolate the role of discretion, Shaffer and colleague looked at changes in prosecutors' charge reductions around sharp changes in mandatory prison laws in North Carolina. Specifically, she said, her group used the North Carolina Sentencing Guidelines,[7] in which defendants with longer criminal records qualify for a mandatory prison sentence while those with the same arrest charge but marginally shorter criminal records do not qualify. For example, Shaffer explained, a defendant who is arrested for selling cocaine and has 15 prior points—a sum of all prior convictions weighted by severity—qualifies for a mandatory prison sentence. A defendant arrested for the same offense but who has only 14 prior points does not qualify. Qualification depends on both the arrest charge and the sum of prior points, said Shaffer, so a prosecutor could reduce a charge such that a defendant would not qualify for a mandatory prison sentence. For defendants who do not qualify for a mandatory prison sentence, a reduction in charge would not impact qualification. By looking at defendants who are just below or just above the 15-point thresholds (i.e., to the left and right of the dotted line at "0 points from discontinuity"), said Shaffer, researchers can isolate prosecutorial discretion. She explained that while the incentive to reduce a charge exists only under one set of circumstances (i.e., to avoid a prison sentence), other reasons for reducing a charge—such as insufficient evidence—are present on both sides.

---

[7] For more information, see Harrington & Shaffer, 2022, p. 36, Figure 2.

Analyzing data from North Carolina, Shaffer and colleagues found a clear, significant increase in charge reductions for individuals who would have otherwise qualified for mandatory prison sentences (Figure 2-5). In other words, for some defendants, prosecutors were exercising their discretion to reduce a defendant's charge, to avoid mandatory prison.

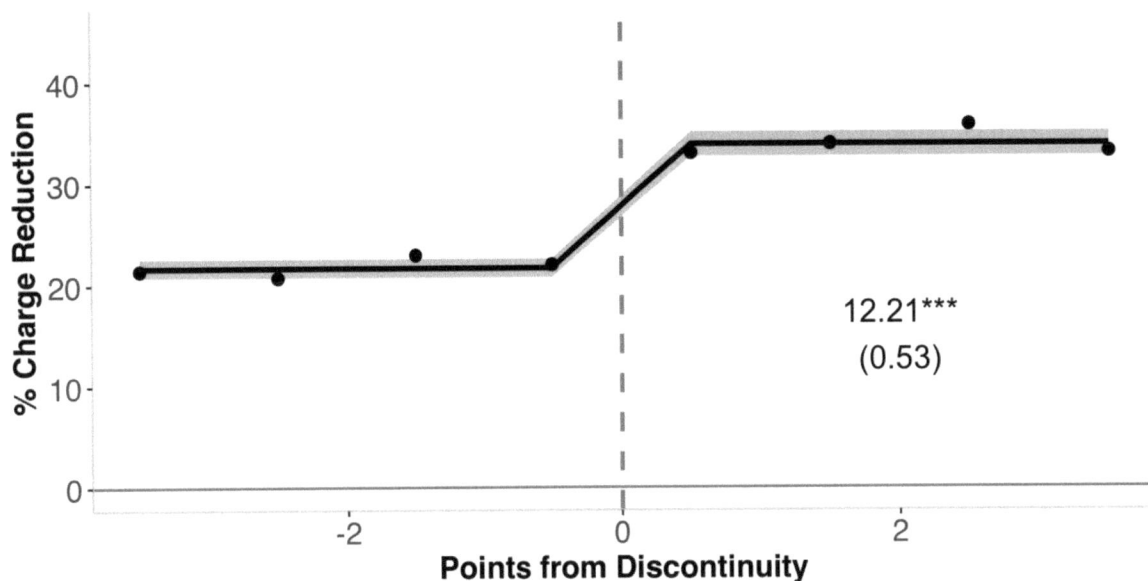

FIGURE 2-5 Aggregate change in charge reductions.
NOTE: This figure depicts prosecutors' charging responses to the mandatory-prison discontinuities in North Carolina's sentencing grids in 1995-2009 and 2010-2019 (the prior-point thresholds for mandatory prison changed in 2010). The x-axis plots the defendant's distance in prior points from a discontinuity given his arrest charge. The y-axis plots the percent of defendants whose arrest charge is reduced. The line and 95% error bands reflect the means in the four points to the right and left of the discontinuities. The annotated coefficient reflects the difference between these averages around the discontinuity. Standard errors are clustered by prosecutor. ***Significant at the 1% level; **5%; *10%.
SOURCE: Harrington & Shaffer, 2022; presentation by Hannah Shaffer on September 23, 2024.

Shaffer and colleagues examined changes in charge reductions over time by race—that is, if prosecutors made different charge reduction decisions based on race, how did these differences change over time? From 1995–2010, Black defendants were significantly more likely to receive charge reductions in circumstances when it did not matter (i.e., when the decision made no difference in whether they qualified for a mandatory prison sentence). This difference could reflect the fact that cases against Black defendants at the arresting stage are weaker on average than for White defendants, said Shaffer. However, Black defendants were less likely to see a charge reduction when it would prevent them from qualifying for a mandatory prison sentence (Figure 2-6). So, between 1995–2010 in North Carolina, prosecutors exercised their discretion in a way that *compounded* existing racial disparities in the criminal justice system, said Shaffer.

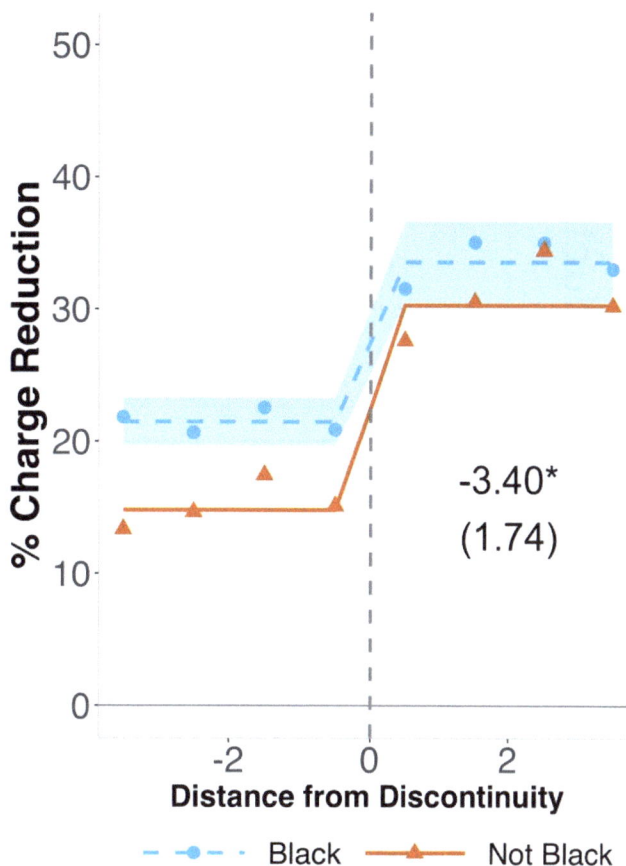

FIGURE 2-6 Compounded disparities from 1995–2010.
NOTE: The x-axis plots defendants' distance from a discontinuity at arrest. The y-axis plots the percent of defendants whose arrest charge is reduced before sentencing. To the right of the dashed line, a charge reduction is necessary to avoid prison. The error bands reflect 95% confidence intervals comparing Black to non-Black defendants, with standard errors clustered by prosecutor. The annotated coefficients report the disparate charging response within four prior points of a discontinuity. *Significant at the 10% level.
SOURCE: Harrington & Shaffer, 2022; presentation by Hannah Shaffer on September 23, 2024.

From 2006–2013, charge reductions were very similar by race on both sides of the dotted line representing discontinuity (Figure 2-7). Prosecutors were more likely to reduce charges when a reduction would help the defendant avoid mandatory prison than when a reduction would not make a difference, but the rate of reduction in both situations was similar for Black and non-

Black defendants. Here, said Shaffer, prosecutors exercised discretion in a way that *passed on* the disparities that already existed in the system, such as higher arrest rates for Black Americans.

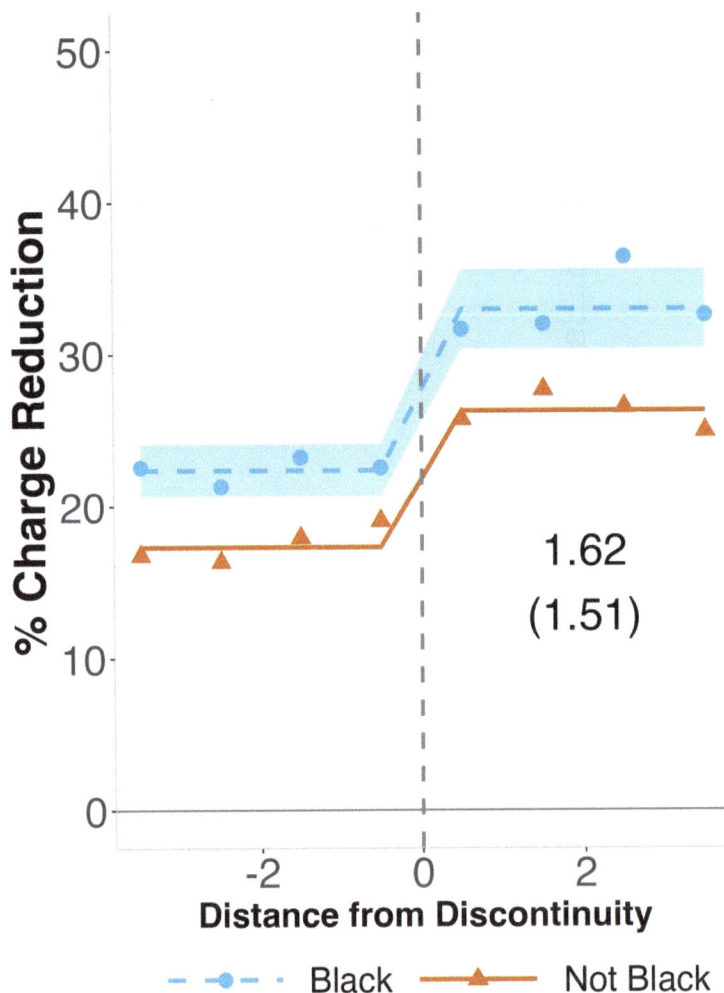

FIGURE 2-7 Passed-through disparities, 2006–2013.
NOTE: The x-axis plots defendants' distance from a discontinuity at arrest. The y-axis plots the percent of defendants whose arrest charge is reduced before sentencing. To the right of the dashed line, a charge reduction is necessary to avoid prison. The error bands reflect 95% confidence intervals comparing Black to non-Black defendants, with standard errors clustered by prosecutor. The annotated coefficients report the disparate charging response within four prior points of a discontinuity.
SOURCE: Harrington & Shaffer, 2022; presentation by Hannah Shaffer on September 23, 2024.

From 2014–2019 a different picture emerged, said Shaffer. During this time, Black defendants were more likely than non-Black defendants to receive a charge reduction when it helped them avoid a mandatory prison sentence (Figure 2-8). Here, she explained, prosecutors exercised their discretion to *offset or reduce* the disparities established at the arrest stage. This trend may contribute to the decline in incarceration disparities, said Shaffer.

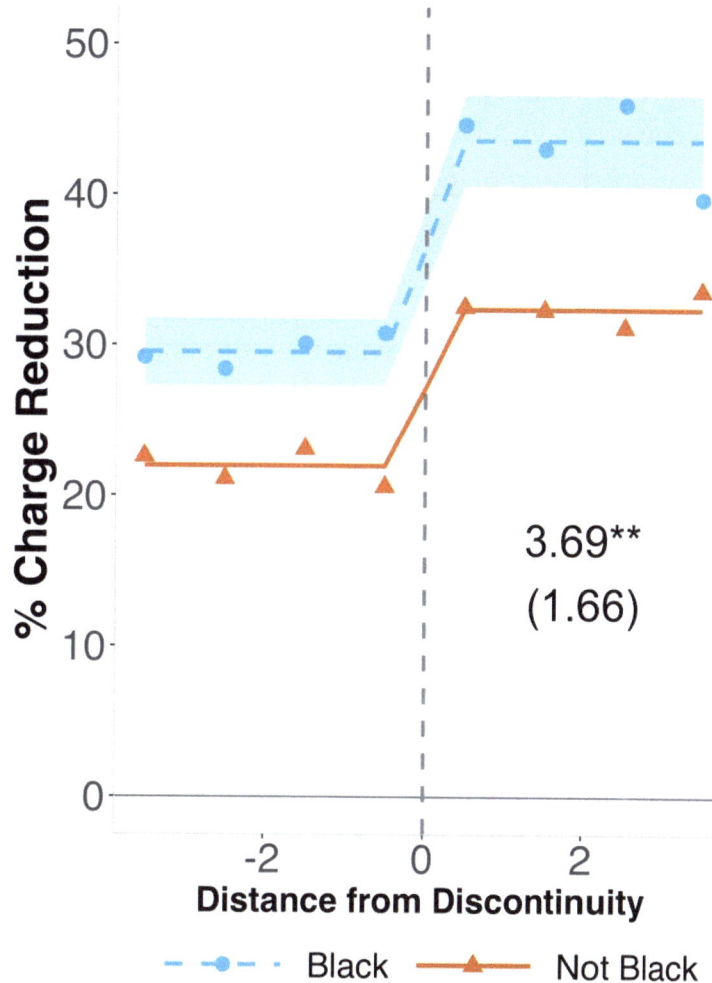

FIGURE 2-8 Offset disparities from 2014–2019.
NOTE: The x-axis plots defendants' distance from a discontinuity at arrest. The y-axis plots the percent of defendants whose arrest charge is reduced before sentencing. To the right of the dashed line, a charge reduction is necessary to avoid prison. The error bands reflect 95% confidence intervals comparing Black to non-Black defendants, with standard errors clustered by prosecutor. The annotated coefficients report the disparate charging response within four prior points of a discontinuity. **Significant at the 5% level.
SOURCE: Harrington & Shaffer, 2022; presentation by Hannah Shaffer on September 23, 2024.

Another potential explanation for the dramatic decline in incarceration disparities, said Shaffer, may be the way prosecutors interpret and respond to the criminal records of Black and White defendants. A very strong association exists between the length of a person's prior criminal record and their likelihood of being sentenced to prison; this is due in part to enhancements for prior convictions, but also to prosecutorial discretion. However, this association was weaker for Black defendants than White defendants, Shaffer said. For defendants with short criminal records, Black and White defendants had similar rates of being sentenced to prison. However, for those with long criminal records, White defendants were significantly more likely to be sentenced to prison than Black defendants. This suggests, said Shaffer, that the sentencing penalty for prior convictions is larger for White defendants.

Shaffer and colleague surveyed prosecutors in North Carolina to understand the empirical patterns they found. The survey presented data on racial disparities in incarceration in North Carolina and asked prosecutors what was driving these disparities. Specifically, the survey asked prosecutors the following: "Among all defendants who are arrested for any felony offense, an average Black defendant receives an active sentence more frequently than an average White defendant. In your view, how important are the following potential explanations in generating this difference?" Prosecutors used a scale from 0–100 to respond to the following options:

- Black defendants tend to have more severe past criminal conduct
- Black defendants tend to have more prior points
- Black defendants tend to have more severe current criminal conduct
- The current conduct of a Black defendant is often perceived to be more serious than the same conduct committed by a White defendant
- Black defendants tend to have lower-quality representation

Shaffer linked prosecutors' responses to these questions to the court cases they handled (Shaffer, 2023). She found that prosecutors who believed disparities were due to differential criminal conduct by Black and White people treated Black and White defendants with similar criminal records similarly; that is, defendants were sentenced to prison at rates commensurate with their prior conviction points, regardless of race. Prosecutors who believed disparities in incarceration were due to bias in the system penalized White defendants more harshly than Black defendants. These differences, said Shaffer, drove the overall racial disparities in penalization of defendants with similar criminal records.

There are several potential ways to interpret these data and to hypothesize why certain prosecutors penalize White defendants more than Black defendants. One potential explanation, Shaffer said, is that prosecutors who perceive bias in the system see prior convictions of Black defendants as less meaningful signals of underlying criminality and instead as reflective of overpolicing or other biases. Prosecutors who see disparities in incarceration as reflecting differing criminal conduct between races, on the other hand, pass through the existing disparities established earlier in the criminal justice process. This work implies that individual prosecutors have enormous power over disparate outcomes, said Shaffer, and that some prosecutors have been exercising their discretion to offset existing disparities.

Promising Practices from Colorado: Reducing Disparities Across Prosecution Decision Points

As noted by other speakers, racial and ethnic disparities exist at various points in the prosecution process. Alexis King, District Attorney for Colorado's First Judicial District, described an effort to address these disparities. Colorado's First Judicial District contains approximately 600,000 people, with a sizeable Latino population (15%) and small Black population (1%). In 2021, King's office set goals to identify disparities, to create a culture of data-driven decision making, and to increase engagement and public accountability. Disparities needed to be addressed in three specific areas, King explained.

First, data showed that, for driving charges that could result in up to $1,000 in fines and up to a year in county jail, White defendants were most likely to have charges dismissed and Hispanic defendants were least likely to have charges dismissed. Second, Hispanic individuals were most likely to plead guilty to low-level drug offenses. Third, Hispanic individuals were most likely to be incarcerated for property crimes, both high-level misdemeanors and low-level felonies. These disparities, said King, reflected both current systematic issues as well as "historical hangovers" in DA polices. While these disparities clearly needed addressing, said King, the types of cases involved did not typically receive much attention from prosecutors.

To make change, said King, efforts to secure support from the prosecutor's office staff were necessary. The first step was to acknowledge and understand the impact of historical policies and practices. For example, prior limitations around deferred judgement and sentences were still influencing current office leadership, she said. Second, support was provided through all-staff training on disparities. A local researcher came to the office to help staff interpret and understand disparities, disproportionality, and systemic drivers. Using a small-group approach with case examples helped with staff engagement, King noted. The third step was to motivate staff by asking middle management to solve problems and invest in change. Although this project began with a small group of high-level leaders said King, it was critical to galvanize the involvement of a larger group. Staff at all levels wanted to improve by altering their practices, King said; asking middle management to support these efforts channeled and capitalized on staff aspirations. The fourth step was to develop policies and practices to respond to identified disparities.

King and the prosecutor's office staff identified several high-priority actions to address disparities. First, for driving and low-level drug possession offenses, they created a system for categorical diversion referrals. Prosecutors worried that this system could devalue their evaluation and discretion, said King, but the data made it clear that a more structured system could decrease disparity in outcomes. Second, the office established working groups to create plea guidance specific to motor vehicle theft and for the use of deferred judgement and sentences. This was the office's first meaningful conversation about property crime, King noted, and it offered an opportunity to break established habits and patterns. The third action involved asking management to focus on property cases and to staff them the same way they would staff more serious crimes, such as aggravated robbery. Fourth, said King, a new data analyst position was created to provide chief deputies with immediate feedback on the impact of new practices on reducing disparities. Finally, the case management system is being reworked to insert equity prompts within case dispositions; the initial step in this process involves adding such prompts to the bond-setting decision-making process. While this system is still in development, King explained, the equity tool will capture systemic drivers when a bond decision is entered. This requirement provides structure to the bond decision, reducing reliance on the DA's discretion. Taken together, said King, these actions will help prosecutors make better-informed decisions, obtain feedback about how cases are being evaluated, and understand which systematic drivers are (or are not) being considered in case resolution.

Discussion on Evidence, Promising Practices, and Racial and Ethnic Disparities

Following panelists' presentations, planning committee members and workshop participants engaged in discussion moderated by Chauhan.

Scalability and Impact on Disparities

While the diversion programs discussed thus far in the workshop seem to have promising results, Chauhan noted, they all involved a small number of individuals. She asked panelists if diversion programs could be successfully scaled up to impact disparities in the criminal justice system, and whether other opportunities might be more promising. In San Francisco, Raphael responded, diversion is used in a small but not insubstantial number of cases—he estimated 10–20 percent. However, because the offenders are overwhelmingly Black and Hispanic, diversion could impact overall disparities. California has seen a significant narrowing of race disparities in incarceration, Raphael said, noting that this narrowing is due to changes in sentencing policy. Changing the "rules that everybody is operating under," rather than relying on discretionary approaches, is likely the best path to reducing disparities, he said.

Rempel agreed that some large jurisdictions can divert a substantial number of cases but expressed his view that other types of policy change may be warranted to significantly impact disparities. For example, mandatory minimum sentences in New York disproportionately impact Black individuals. If these laws were changed, reducing racial disparities would be "mathematically inevitable." While these initial programs are small, Epperson said, they can produce evidence that can be used to impact many more people. For example, Epperson and his colleagues researched a misdemeanor deferred prosecution program that was "extremely light touch,"[8] consisting of only two sessions, and most participants did not recidivate. The effectiveness of a diversion program that does "almost nothing" suggests that prosecutors could decline to prosecute these types of cases and see similar results, he said.

Dependence on Prosecutors

Foxx observed that prosecutor-led diversion programs, by definition, rely on the discretion of individual prosecutors. She asked panelists to comment on how diversion programs can continue to succeed following changes in administration. Mallory responded that the solution lies in data and education. For example, Mallory and his colleagues found that most individuals facing gun charges are not involved in drugs or gangs and are instead looking to protect themselves and their families. By sharing these data and educating the community, the community can advocate for change and encourage prosecutors to use alternative approaches.

---

[8] For a description of the program, see Epperson et al., 2023.

Evidence-Based Practice

Agan asked panelists for their thoughts on striking a balance between implementing evidence-based policies, innovating and trying new programs and responses, and generating evidence on a program's effectiveness. Available literature predominately contains studies of people charged with nonviolent offenses and studies comparing traditional prosecution to diversion, Rempel responded. However, he said, some new programs are not yet backed by sufficient evidence, including programs that dismiss cases altogether and diversion for cases involving violence, such as the gun diversion model discussed during the session. Although these new models are promising, it would be a "misimpression to communicate that we already have a lot of evidence on current models," Raphael said. He added that the ability to generate evidence is often conditional on access to both data and to DA's offices that are willing to partner with researchers and experiment with their methods, even if the research "shows things that they do not like." However, he noted that opportunities exist for researchers to be creative and to find natural experiments through which they can study causal questions. Mallory agreed that generating data requires collaborating with prosecutors who are willing to take risks. Although existing evidence is limited, sharing preliminary research with prosecutors can provide ideas about alternatives to prosecution and can help them make informed decisions about programs to implement, Mallory said.

PROSECUTORIAL PERSPECTIVES: CHALLENGES AND OPPORTUNITIES FOR IMPLEMENTATION

Following the sessions highlighting research findings and promising practices, Marlene Biener, Association of Prosecuting Attorneys and workshop planning committee member, led panelists in a roundtable discussion to highlight perspectives from prosecutors and nonprofit leaders working closely with prosecutors on program implementation.

Prosecutor Perspective: Florida's 17th Circuit

Florida's 17th circuit, in Broward County, has over 2 million residents and the 16th largest prosecutor's office in the United States, said Harold Pryor, State Attorney for Florida's 17th Judicial Circuit. The county is highly diverse, with approximately one-third White residents, one-third Black residents, and one-third Hispanic residents. The prosecutor's office prosecutes crimes ranging from minor misdemeanors to first-degree premeditated murder, said Pryor; recent efforts aim to reduce incarceration and disparities without compromising community safety. In Broward County, most people who are accused of crimes are people of color or people with lower socioeconomic status. Their reasons for committing crimes could include lack of economic opportunities, lack of educational opportunities, mental health or drug addiction issues, or a combination of factors. When Pryor took office in 2021, he felt compelled to create programs offering opportunities in each of these areas. Diversion programs and specialized courts already existed for mental health and drug addiction, he said, but no programs aimed at addressing the lack of economic and educational opportunities. To address these issues despite a limited budget and limited opportunities beyond incarceration, Pryor reached out to community partners and organizations that had the resources and tools to offer the economic and educational opportunities people were missing.

The first program created, said Pryor, was in partnership with an organization that aimed to train and employ people coming out of the criminal justice system. Despite receiving $2 million from the Department of Labor, the organization struggled to identify individuals eligible to receive the services. Pryor and the organization's chief executive officer created a program called Economic Empowerment Today, in which people accused of committing nonviolent felony offenses can receive a certification and job-finding assistance.[9] Upon program completion, an individual's offense is downgraded to a nonfelony or dismissed entirely. This program, said Pryor, allows people to leave the criminal justice system not as convicted felons, but as people with gainful employment and a sense of pride.

A similar program, the Court to College Program, was created for individuals hoping to pursue educational opportunities.[10] Through this program, individuals who commit nonviolent offenses can earn a GED, obtain an associate's degree, and/or become certified or licensed for a skilled job. Program completion leads to downgrading or dismissal of the case. Again, said Pryor, participants can leave the criminal justice system with advanced education and improved employment opportunities. These programs are also available to victims of crimes, who in general, may be at risk of future criminal justice system involvement, said Pryor.

---

[9] For more information, see https://browardsao.com/diversion-programs/

[10] For more information, see https://browardsao.com/diversion-programs/

Another new program, said Pryor, is directed at cases in which children have been accused of domestic violence. The program serves everyone impacted by the incident, including the child, parents, and others in the home. Community members help develop an "Integrated Family Safety Plan" that offers services and support to the entire family; this could include support for mental health, drug addiction, or lack of economic or educational opportunities. Recidivism rates among youth who completed this program decreased substantially, said Pryor, and families received the support they need.

"This is how we are trying to reimagine the criminal justice system," said Pryor, by holistically examining the multiple, intertwined issues that lead to crime and finding solutions to those issues. While the criminal justice system itself is not equipped to solve every problem, he said, partnering with other stakeholders can make it possible to address people's needs and reverse the cycle of crime.

Prosecutor Perspective: Ramsey County

John Choi, County Attorney for Ramsey, Minnesota, explained his unintentional entry into the prosecution field. In his previous job as City Attorney, he prosecuted lower-level misdemeanor and gross misdemeanor adult crimes. New to the position, Choi said that he gravitated toward the prosecution function of the job in attempt to better understand the position. His lack of prior experience in prosecution was beneficial, he said, as it allowed him to more easily see issues in the system, such as a lack of data-driven practices and the pursuit of outcomes that were not in the public's interest. In this role, Choi used data and created diversion programs; he was elected as County Attorney in 2010. Historically, the criminal justice system has suffered from a lack of critical thought about its intended function, and a lack of research on the impacts of its practices, said Choi.

The biggest challenge in prosecution is thinking beyond the current adversarial system, said Choi. Less than two percent of cases go to a jury trial while the rest, he said, are addressed through a plea-bargaining process that is "like an assembly line"—it processes people toward a form of conviction, which often leads to further involvement with the criminal legal system. In 2019, in attempt to think outside of the adversarial system, Choi and his colleagues implemented a program called (Re)Imagining Justice for Youth.[11] This program aims to find community-based solutions, particularly within those communities most impacted by crime and the criminal legal system. A leadership team was created to "unpack" the adversarial system and to consider ways to make prosecution more collaborative. For example, in the traditional system, the prosecutor often makes charging decisions based solely on information from police, rather than gathering additional information that could help them better understand the human context and individual needs in specific cases, he said. In place of the traditional model in which the prosecutor is the sole decision maker, the program's leadership team developed a collaborative model, with a multidisciplinary review team to make case decisions. This collaborative review team includes the prosecutor, the public defender, and the community. To decide whether to offer the community-based accountability alternative, the collaborative review team first engages with the youth's family to learn more about their situation and the reasons for their involvement with the criminal justice system. The team decides among four potential options. First, a case can be returned to the family, along with support and resources to help them resolve it. Second, a case can be referred to a community-based accountability program, in which community providers use a restorative justice model. Third, a petition can be filed asking for a judge's involvement but asking that the judge allow the community to help resolve the case. Finally, the case can be filed in the traditional youth justice court system.

When this program was launched, said Choi, it experienced pushback from prosecutors, because asking prosecutors to share decision-making power represented a fundamental change in thinking. However, said Choi, this informed decision-making model has erased racial disparities in success rates for alternative programs, such as the new community-based accountability approach, compared to prior diversion programs the office utilized.

PERSPECTIVES ON IMPLEMENTATION FROM RESEARCHER-PRACTITIONER PARTNERSHIPS

Carrie Pettus shared her work at Wellbeing & Equity Innovations, a national nonprofit translational research firm that seeks to impact the criminal justice field by bridging practice and research. Pettus focused her remarks on efforts to research the effectiveness of trauma-

---

[11] For more information, see https://www.ramseycounty.us/your-government/leadership/county-attorneys-office/reimagining-justice-youth

responsive diversion programming. One project, based in Indianapolis, is a randomized controlled trial of a trauma-responsive diversion program that specifically serves individuals who were victims of nonfatal shooting incidents and who, within a year, became defendants. The goal of this project is to prevent future victimization and future offending by treating and intervening in trauma, which has been empirically shown to be related to future threats to both the individual and the public.[12] This program, said Pettus, "challenges our notion of who are victims and defendants in our communities." The second project, based in New Jersey, has a similar focus on violence prevention and retaliation prevention, using a trauma-responsive diversion approach.[13] This program is currently undergoing feasibility and acceptability testing. Key implementation components for both programs included engagement with community members, community partners, stakeholders within the prosecutor's office, and neighborhood associations and advocacy groups, said Pettus. Building significant stakeholder support stabilizes these types of programs, she stated.

Mona Sahaf introduced herself as the director of the Reshaping Prosecution Initiative at the Vera Institute of Justice, a large criminal justice nonprofit. Prior to her current role, Sahaf served as a prosecutor at the U.S. Attorney's Office for the District of Columbia and the Department of Justice (DOJ) in the Human Rights & Special Prosecution Section. As part of her job at DOJ, she traveled the country and observed how prosecutors charge, how defense attorneys operate, and how judges' sentencing varies depending on region. This perspective informs her work at Vera, Sahaf noted. Sahaf's team consists of former trial attorneys, public defenders, and prosecutors, as well as qualitative and quantitative researchers, community organizers, and teachers. The initiative focuses primarily on building diversion programs. In their current model, a DA's office and a community-based organization apply jointly to work with the Vera Institute of Justice; an existing relationship between the two, as well as community support, are required. Approved applicants receive technical assistance and guidance for building programs with a race equity lens. The Vera Institute of Justice aims to work with community-based organizations that are "Black, Brown, or system-impacted-led, or deeply embedded in these communities," she said, noting that the program includes sustainability efforts. Building an

---

[12] For more information see https://wellbeingandequity.org/wp-content/uploads/2024/09/INDY-TID-One-pager.pdf

[13] For information see https://wellbeingandequity.org/wpcontent/uploads/2024/09/APPO_About_WEI_vf_121123.pdf

effective program takes more than a year, said Sahaf, and Vera Institute cannot "parachute into jurisdictions" and then leave. In exchange for Vera Institute's assistance with program implementation, the partners agree to share data to evaluate the program's impact.

Based on her experience at Vera, Sahaf shared three reflections about the current state of prosecution. First, interest in implementing changes, particularly related to diversion, is incredibly high in diverse communities all over the country. Second, the prosecution field has an ongoing need to measure program outcomes. Data collection continues to be a big challenge, and many actors are hesitant to share data. Data are essential to this work, she said, because well-communicated evidence is necessary to inform the public's understanding of how to achieve public safety. Finally, racial disparities exist in the criminal justice system due to multiple intersectional issues with long historical legacies. While prosecutors and others can take steps to reduce these disparities, additional frameworks and resources are needed to fully address root causes, she said.

IMPLEMENTATION CHALLENGES AND OPPORTUNITIES

Biener noted that workshop speakers highlighted several challenges to implementing prosecutorial programs that see to reduce racial disparities or provide alternatives to incarceration, such as limited resources, budgetary constraints, and the need for greater buy-in. Speakers also identified solutions to these challenges, such as partnering with external stakeholders who can provide the necessary resources.

One major contributor to success, said Pettus, involves the prosecutor's office trusting community partners and family systems with responsibilities, rather than trying to manage programs by themselves. The two biggest challenges for prosecutors are finding partners who deliver evidence-based services and working to cultivate a culture of trust with those partners and the community, Pettus said. Another important success factor involves acknowledging that contact with the criminal legal system impacts not only the accused person but also their family. Focusing on the family system is critical, Pryor noted. When his own family members were victimized, they did not get the level of care that others would have received because they were Black and poor, said Pryor—which explains why marginalized communities often lack trust in the criminal justice system. Pryor said, "Every day, my job is to…work towards rebuilding or gaining trust with our community."

Pettus and Pryor also discussed the role of trust between prosecutors and researchers. It is the responsibility of researchers, said Pettus, to earn that trust by acknowledging the daily realities of prosecutorial practice, and by communicating and contextualizing their learnings in ways that are useful for prosecutors. Partnering with research organizations requires trust from prosecutors, Pryor said, particularly in terms of trusting that data will be treated with integrity. When Pryor's office partnered with the Prosecutorial Performance Indicator (PPI) project,[14] some staff worried that shared information would be used to punish them if they took certain actions. Pryor said that sharing information with PPI is a way for the office to hold itself collectively accountable. Sharing allows the office to look at their data honestly and to make changes in response to that data, to ensure a more fair, just, and equitable criminal justice system. Further, said Pryor, the data dashboards created for the public allow communities to view information in real time and to hold the office accountable; being open and transparent contributes to earning the community's trust.

Reducing Racial and Ethnic Disparities

Diversion programs and other alternatives to incarceration are often designed with the intention of reducing racial and ethnic disparities, said Biener. However, while these alternatives may reduce overall incarceration numbers, racial and ethnic disparities are sometimes maintained or even exacerbated. Biener asked panelists to comment on implementing programs that are effective for public safety and also effective at reducing racial disparities.

All the Vera Institute of Justice's programs are built to center race equity, with the goal of removing cases from the system, said Sahaf. In addition, programs do not exclude people based on prior criminal history. This is a bold change in many jurisdictions, acknowledged Sahaf—most current diversion programs, including some of the new programs presented by workshop speakers, are only for individuals facing charges for the first time or for low-level offences, she noted. Collecting, analyzing, and sharing data are critical to making changes that do not exacerbate racial and ethnic disparities, said Sahaf. She shared an example of a low-level drug diversion program that was effective at reducing disparities. The program involved a close partnership between police and prosecutors; police were instructed to transfer low-level drug cases to the diversion program. The total number of misdemeanor drug cases fell significantly

---

[14] For more information, see https://prosecutorialperformanceindicators.org/

over several years, from approximately 20 percent of the case load down to about 5 percent. Racial disparities lessened as well, said Sahaf. At the beginning, Black individuals were approximately 5.7 times more likely to be charged with a misdemeanor drug case, and this dropped to 2.7 percent. Low-level drug diversion is a way to take many cases out of the system and reduce disparities, she concluded.

Disparities in felony cases are often more challenging to address, said Sahaf. Black people are approximately 10 times more likely than White people to receive a felony drug charge, and far more public support is available for diversion programs aimed at individuals facing charges for lower-level offences. There is less appetite for offering diversion to individuals with multiple prior arrests and convictions, and perhaps those who have been assigned diversion previously. However, said Sahaf, these may be the individuals who are most in need of a diversion program. All prosecutors have seen individuals and families who cycle in and out of the criminal justice system, she said—"the cycle of violence is painted in the surnames on these dockets." Sahaf noted the importance of diverting more challenging cases, including those of individuals with criminal histories, individuals who have previously not succeeded in diversion, and individuals who have weapons charges in addition to drug charges. People of color and lower-income people are more likely to have prior criminal history contacts, she said, so expanding services to more challenging cases is the only way to significantly reduce racial disparities. Diversion opportunities are often offered only to people with no criminal history or people who can afford the cost of the program. Racial disparities will persist until these opportunities are offered equitably, said Sahaf.

Choi said that data analysis in his office showed that racial disparities in the cases initially brought to the prosecutor's office remained similar at each decision point as the cases moved through the criminal justice system. By increasing their awareness of the details of the cases before them, prosecutors can make deliberate, intentional efforts to reduce disparities, he noted. Often, the sense among prosecutors is that they are supposed to treat all people similarly, often illustrated as "lady justice with a blindfold on." The truth, said Choi, is that "we have to actually rip off the blindfold" to achieve racial equity.

Prosecutors can also influence events that occur before a case reaches them, said Choi. For example, in Ramsey County, Minnesota Black individuals are four times more likely to be pulled over for a non-public-safety traffic stop, and nine times more likely to be subjected to a search compared to White motorists. Choi raised this issue with the police and his community; in response, some police agencies in his district agreed to reduce non-public-safety traffic stops, choosing instead to use their limited resources to focus on violations like speeding and driving under the influence. After enacting this change, said Choi, disparities in traffic stops and associated searches dropped significantly.

As an example of a program that has been successful in reducing racial disparities, Choi raised the previously discussed collaborative review team program used for youth facing charges. Prior to this program, large disparities existed in terms of who was offered alternatives to prosecution and who was successful at these alternatives. "We said out loud that these disparities…are not okay," said Choi. By using a team approach and including the voices of the victim, the individual, and the family, opportunities and successes were more equitable. For example, Choi explained that some youth previously failed the alternative program because their families did not attend the first required meeting. Engaging with the family before deciding the fate of a case led to a dramatic turnaround in terms of which individuals were offered the program and which succeeded. Biener commented on a recurring theme in this discussion—the importance of partnerships with external stakeholders. "It is very difficult to do this work in a silo and to be effective," she said.

Pettus emphasized the importance of engaging with criminal justice system-impacted communities when planning programs designed to address racial disparities. A significant number of people in marginalized communities only experience the criminal justice system as "adversarial and harmful and hurtful," she said. When offered a diversion program from this system, "why would they all of a sudden want to participate?" It is important for prosecutors to engage in significant trust-building efforts and communication with these communities from the beginning, said Pettus. Without this trust, individuals from certain communities may decline to participate in alternatives to incarceration, thus maintaining or exacerbating racial disparities. Instead of blaming individuals for declining to participate, she said, program designers could benefit from considering the potentially unpalatable aspects of their solutions.

Engaging Victims

In the criminal justice system, victims and defendants are usually considered to be two separate categories, said Biener; but the situation is more complex. Biener asked panelists how to consider prior victimization when working with defendants, and how the criminal justice system can engage victims. Pettus explained that her work challenges the bifurcated notion of victims and defendants. Many defendants have previously been victims, particularly in cases of gun violence, but they are often not considered victims. When prosecutors shift their thinking to consider the harm and trauma many defendants suffered prior to their offenses, said Pettus, both defendants' outcomes and public safety could improve. Depending on the study and the types of psychological trauma, research has found that approximately 99 percent of people in prison have had prior traumatic experiences; in jail populations, this ranges from 60–70 percent (Pettus, 2023). Remarkably, she said, the overwhelming majority of this trauma occurred within 30 days prior to the individuals' arrests (Tripodi et al., n.d.). Prosecutors would do well to keep the immediate impacts of trauma in mind when engaging with victims, and to work with community partners to offer supportive mental health care and trauma treatment. If trauma remains unaddressed, said Pettus, victims may become defendants, cycling in and out of the criminal justice system.

Sahaf expanded on the power of engaging victims in the criminal legal process. The system is not designed to serve victims, she said, other than through their limited role of providing testimony and giving a victim impact statement. Victims who have completed restorative justice programs have powerfully noted supports they did not receive from the criminal legal system and supports they *did* receive from restorative justice, including help with healing from trauma. Choi added that, historically, many prosecutors have considered themselves to be working on behalf of victims, with the belief that the offender's punishment and incarceration would heal the victim's wounds. However, the process is often far more transactional: the victim simply shows up in the courtroom as expected, and the offender is convicted and held accountable. Courtroom events and the case outcome are "not really a part of the healing journey" for the victim, he said. Despite feeling heard, a victim may not feel they have received the services they want and need. The job of a prosecutor, Choi emphasized, is not just to do right by the victim, but also to do right by the community, including those who are accused of crimes. Instead of approaching crime with a one-size-fits-all adversarial system, it is important for prosecutors to critically examine whether the current process produces the desired outcomes, or whether alternatives may be more effective.

Building a Culture of Sustainability

Biener asked panelists how policies and programs like those discussed during the workshop can be sustained over time, particularly in the face of staff turnover and administration changes. Pryor said that many veteran prosecutors have similar frustrations with the "hard reality" of the system—previously incarcerated individuals return to the system with their criminal behavior unchanged. Pryor leverages these shared experiences to talk with veteran prosecutors about the importance of working with researchers and using data to develop a better approach. "We've been doing it wrong for so long—let's try something else," said Pryor. Most prosecutors want to hold people accountable, ensure safer communities, and work within a fair, equitable system. Conversations about system shortcomings can get veteran prosecutors to "buy in," said Pryor.

Pryor also works to engage the community—creating relationships and motivating community support can help ensure sustainability. Growing up, Pryor said that he and his friends only knew what prosecutors were if they were accused of a crime—prosecutors did not visit their neighborhood. Pryor's office has an incentive program to encourage prosecutors and their support staff to interact with communities by participating in conversations about how they are working to protect the rights of all people, including those accused of crimes.

Prosecutors have a difficult job, said Pettus. Paraphrasing a Los Angeles prosecutor, Pettus noted that prosecutors make daily "life-and-death" decisions with no correct answer— they may either take away someone's freedom or let that person back on the streets where they may hurt someone. Pettus encouraged chief prosecutors to build an office culture that acknowledges the difficulty of the job and supports prosecutors and staff. Furthermore, she said, it is important to build an office culture in which people share success stories about diversion— sharing these stories with other prosecutors and with the public allows everyone to acknowledge and celebrate the hard work and success.

3

Data Use and Data Culture in Prosecutors' Offices

Besiki Kutateladze, Florida International University and workshop planning committee member, moderated a panel discussion on data use and data culture in prosecutors' offices. Partnerships between researchers and prosecutors are essential for gathering data on practices, outcomes, racial disparities, and other measures of interest, Kutateladze said.

Kutateladze noted that prosecutors' offices have different models for data analysis, ranging from one prosecutor doing data work to a dedicated research and analytical unit. Trust between prosecutors and researchers is essential, Kutateladze added, with the caveat that a researcher's job is not to "only deliver good news," but to support and improve policies and practices. Kutateladze then introduced the session's panelists and asked them a series of questions about the current state of data use and data culture in prosecutors' offices.

Data are just the beginning of the process of data-driven decision making, said Don Stemen, Loyola University of Chicago. Data can be used to diagnose a problem, and diagnosis leads to discussion about how to address that problem. The discussion may indicate the need for additional data to support a policy or program. For a prosecutor's office to become a data-driven organization, said Stemen, the office needs infrastructure to support data collection, analysis, and use. Prosecution data have several challenges, many of which stem from the collection of criminal justice data by many agencies in many different systems. Data compatibility is "incredibly problematic," said Stemen, and often data are not in the format or at the level of detail that prosecutors need—data may be insufficiently defined or poorly documented. Case management systems are proprietary, and systems used by other agencies may not permit data sharing. Furthermore, said Stemen, case management systems are built to manage cases, not as data-analysis tools.

For data to be helpful, a data-use plan is necessary, he stated. In addition to challenges with data availability and quality, data use in many offices is hindered by a lack of analytic capacity. Smaller jurisdictions may still use paper files or antiquated case management systems.

43

Data analysis and use often occur only within an executive team and may lack a clear connection to office goals. Prosecutors may not see data as a decision-making tool but instead as a means of oversight, said Stemen.

Measures for Justice is a nonprofit organization with the goal of bringing data transparency to the criminal justice system, said Gipsy Escobar, Measures for Justice. A national data portal contains core data on the performance of the criminal justice system from 20 states and 1,200 counties, said Escobar. The organization has worked with communities, to allow them to engage with the data, and with prosecutors, to create and track policy goals. Further, Measures for Justice developed tools to evaluate the data culture, data infrastructure, and data quality in prosecutors' offices. Through a partnership with the Association for Prosecuting Attorneys, aiming to collect data from 10 prosecutors' offices, Measures for Justice identified several common data challenges. One challenge involves missing information across fields; for example, at one site, 90 percent of cases were missing judge information. Escobar noted that there are artificial intelligence (AI) tools in development to analyze judges' decision-making patterns; however, these tools are ineffective if 90 percent of the necessary data are missing. Invalid values are another common challenge; this happens when the information entered in a field does not fall into one of the assigned value categories. Systems also exhibited inconsistent case outcomes, said Escobar, with cases being marked as "open" but with all charges dismissed. In addition, event dates were sometimes improperly recorded—11 percent of cases had an arrest date that preceded the incident date. Finally, many cases, such as expunged or declined cases, are removed from datasets. All these missing or incorrect data hinder the ability to use data to inform and guide practice, said Escobar.

Oren Gur, director of the District Attorney's Transparency Analytics (DATA) Lab, Philadelphia's District Attorney's (DA) Office, said using data teams, developing data-informed policy, researching policy and practice, and influencing public discourse through data are all emerging areas of focus for prosecutors. Multiple agencies within the criminal justice system generate and use data. Police generate data on incidents and arrests, prosecutors on charges and cases, and courts on outcomes, he said. Prosecutors may have access to both police and court data and can combine these data to systematically examine current trends and practices. However, prosecutors' offices have been historically underresourced and underleveraged from a data and research perspective, limiting this ability. In Philadelphia, the DATA Lab works within the DA's office to "use data, research, and advocacy to inform policies and practices; increase equity, transparency, and accountability; and reduce harms through prosecutorial and systems reform in Philadelphia and beyond." Gur called attention to the phrase "and beyond," noting that learnings from Philadelphia can be applied more broadly. One objective of the DATA Lab is to become an integral component of the DA's office; Gur said that such institutionalization is essential for sustainability. The DATA Lab received initial funding from foundations but is working to procure additional funding. The daily work of the DATA Lab falls into five areas, said Gur: operations, research, policy/practice, transparency, and community. This multipronged approach allows shifts in capacity, to focus on areas in need of extra attention, he said.

Aurélie Ouss, University of Pennsylvania, described how collaborations between criminal justice researchers and prosecutors' offices can improve programs, policies, and practices. The research partnership between University of Pennsylvania and the Philadelphia DA's office, established in 2020, has several goals, said Ouss. The first goal involves understanding the role prosecutors play in shaping criminal justice outcomes, and the effects of policies such as cash bail reform or diversion programs. Second, the partnership aims to develop data opportunities, both for graduate students and for researchers outside of the University of Pennsylvania. For example, several researchers are embedded within the DA's office and can access all data available to prosecutors, said Ouss; they can develop their own research agendas around prosecution and criminal justice. Third, beyond prosecution, the partnership is leveraging this collaboration to improve understanding of how penal decisions are shaped. Prosecutors are central to many processes, she explained, because they receive data from both police departments and courts, and they generate their own data through their case management systems.

One critical aspect of the partnership is the dissemination of the work. Ouss gave an example of research conducted and disseminated to address an issue within the criminal justice system. Ouss and her colleague researched bail reform (Ouss & Stevenson, 2023) and noticed that the term "Failure to Appear" (FTA) was associated not just with defendants but often with other court actors such as police officers, victims, civilian witnesses, or defense attorneys. The team dug deeper into court records to understand the scale of this issue, said Ouss, and found that nondefendants were far more likely to miss court than defendants (Graef et al., 2024). For example, defendants missed at least one court hearing in 19 percent of cases; by contrast, police officers missed court in 30 percent of cases they were ordered to attend. In addition, Ouss and colleague found that cases in which at least one witness missed court were twice as likely to be dismissed as cases in which no one missed court; in fact, witness FTA is the most significant predictor of a case being dropped—more so than charge, criminal history, and demographics combined. Ouss and colleagues presented their findings internally to the prosecutor's office, working with unit supervisors to present results in the most understandable format, including simple visuals. Alongside the DATA Lab, they conducted research-to-action meetings to help disseminate results internally and externally. The results did not surprise prosecutors, she said, but providing data helped elevate the issue. The work has continued, said Ouss, through monthly meetings with stakeholder groups who are working to address the issue. This example illustrates how doing research with the DA's office can help elevate issues that reach beyond the office and can help bring stakeholders together to work on improving the criminal justice system, said Ouss.

Researchers can engage in mutually beneficial collaborations with DA offices in multiple ways, said Ouss. When DA offices give researchers access to data, researchers can both answer important academic and policy questions and find ways to make data and data analysis helpful to prosecutors' daily work. DA offices may be unsure how to use much of the data they collect, and researchers can help organize and interpret these data to help prosecutors identify challenges and develop solutions. Data analysis may, in turn, reveal areas in which more data collection would be helpful to provide a clearer understanding of criminal justice system dynamics and operations. The first step in this collaboration, said Ouss, is for researchers to take time to listen to and understand the office's needs and questions. Once researchers understand the office's needs, they can use available data or collect new data, translating these data into formats helpful to all stakeholders, from defendants to victims to prosecutors.

Ann Davison, City Attorney for Seattle, Washington. is the city's independently elected prosecutor, overseeing the criminal division with 80 attorneys and staff and the civil division with 110 attorneys and staff. The criminal division receives approximately 10,000–12,000 gross and simple misdemeanor referrals for prosecution each year from the Seattle Police Department. Davison presented two case studies of challenges in Seattle and described the approach she and her office took to address those challenges.

The first challenge, said Davison, was a backlog of undecided cases that had been growing for years. When she took office, there were some data available but no comprehensive data-collection effort. With a one-person data shop, Davison's office began to compile data to identify the points at which cases were delayed, and to determine how decision-making processes could be changed to clear the backlog. While other actors within the criminal justice system may also have contributed to delays, Davison noted, she focused on areas in which she could make changes. One of the first changes Davison made was to implement a close-in-time policy, in which a decision to decline, divert, or charge a case needed to be made relatively quickly. Previously, some cases remained without a decision for more than a year; this was not helpful for victims, defense counsel, or defendants, she said. Making a decision within a short time of an alleged criminal act demonstrates responsiveness to the community, said Davison. This new policy began to impact the backlog, although later staffing issues caused a small increase. She reported that the median time to make a filing decision dropped from a high of 111 days in 2021 to 7 days in 2022 and 16 days in 2023.

A second challenge Davison faced was how to address open-air drug markets in parts of Seattle. Davison's office used data on criminal referrals, overdose deaths, service centers, and community input to make hotspot maps of the drug market areas. Based on these hotspot maps, the city council passed an ordinance to implement targeted interventions, such as emergency shelters, clinics, and permanent housing. Davison noted that the data used for the analysis, the legislation passed, and the interventions implemented required the support of multiple government agencies and community partners. Each branch of government and each sector plays a role in addressing such issues; a prosecutor's office cannot be responsible for fixing every social issue, she said.

Multnomah County, Oregon, is a medium-sized jurisdiction that serves 800,000 residents in eight cities with four police agencies, said Caroline Wong, Deputy District Attorney for Multnomah County. The DA's office employs 100 attorneys and 255 staff and prosecutes both misdemeanor and felony cases. The office data team consists of one attorney lead, three research and evaluation analysts, and two graduate-level interns. When DA Mike Schmidt took office in 2020, one of his first priorities was to implement data-driven decision making and transparency, she said. Over the past four years, the office has developed public-facing dashboards to promote data sharing; the website includes a dashboard user guide, a criminal justice systems map, a data-tracking definitions document, and a timeline of policy and process changes to help provide context to the data. The team has also focused on data literacy, said Wong, by providing trainings and community presentations, and has taken steps to grow the office's data culture by increasing data accessibility and incorporating feedback from community members and practitioners. The goal, she said, is for prosecutor's office attorneys and staff to have the data they need to do their jobs well.

Wong explained that she serves as a bridge between the practices of prosecution and data analytics. She was assigned to work with nontraditional diversion programs and found herself collaborating with outside researchers to ensure that alternatives to traditional prosecution were effective. Wong said she learned that collaboration and communication with other prosecutors and the community are essential. Rather than just asking a DA to collect data for a project, it is better to sit with the DA to explain the process and why the information is needed, she said. Similarly, Wong spent time listening to the community to find out which types of information they would find meaningful, so the office could collect and share these data. Meaningful, two-way communication about data needs is important, she said. For example, the data team can ask prosecutors which kinds of data could make their jobs easier, either in the process of prosecution or in talking with victims and the community. Obtaining feedback from practitioners and gathering and sharing relevant data, said Wong, have been powerful ways to build data culture and to secure support from practitioners.

PROSECTUOR'S OFFICE: COOK COUNTY

In an earlier workshop session, DA Kimberly Foxx shared that her approach to prosecution involves using data to show results. When she was first elected in 2016, Foxx said she knew that constituents would want to see results of the changes made during her term. Her office built open data portals to collect and share county-wide crime and justice information. While data and research are essential for making evidence-based changes, Foxx said, data are not always valued—instead, people tend to rely on whether they feel safe.

Working with researchers to collect data is essential for making policy changes, said Foxx, because "you cannot fix what you cannot measure." However, such work requires lawyers to exhibit a level of humility, said Foxx. Tension can exist between the lawyer's real-life experiences and the researcher's academic expertise. Foxx gave an example from her early career illustrating the importance of working with researchers. Researchers were working to analyze the composition of the county jail population and the underlying reasons for their incarceration. Data showed that many people who were in jail were there because they could not afford bail. It was Foxx's job to explain the research to other actors in the criminal legal system and the community.

Chicago has an array of academic institutions that are eager to work with prosecutors and others to conduct research on the criminal legal system, said Foxx. Over the past eight years, the field of prosecution has embraced data and formed research-practice partnerships. This demonstrates an emerging acknowledgement among prosecutors, said Foxx, that "we cannot practice the way that we've practiced before"—instead, it is important to engage with research and be thoughtful in the work. Prosecution is a risk-averse field, she said, and prosecutors might worry that research could show that their policies are not having the intended effect, or that findings of unfairness or racism might suggest that individuals working in the criminal justice system are themselves unfair or racist. Relying on research rather than anecdotal evidence is not the traditional culture of prosecution, said Foxx. However, over the last few years, this culture has started to shift as prosecutors begin to engage in research. "Institutional bravery" is needed to continue the evidence-based prosecution approach, said Foxx.

DATA ON RACE AND ETHNICITY

In a workshop session focused on data use and data culture in prosecutors' offices (see Appendix B), Kutateladze asked panelists to comment on how race and ethnicity data are captured. Stemen replied that, in most jurisdictions he works with, race and ethnicity data are captured by law enforcement and transferred to prosecutors' offices when the case is referred. Some offices have tried to confirm these data by cross-checking it against other available data. For example, he said, last names can be checked against census records and classified as Latino if an individual's last name is among those for which 85 percent or more people self-identify as Latino. Driver's license records can also be used to cross-check; linking with the Department of Motor Vehicles' records allows access to race and ethnicity data self-identified by individuals. Escobar agreed that, in her experience, most race and ethnicity data come from the arresting officer. Prosecutors generally have little contact with the defendant outside of court, she noted, resulting in a lack of opportunity to collect data firsthand. Gur suggested that, in addition to linking records, AI could accelerate the process of classifying complex race and ethnicity data. Escobar added that challenges exist when using technology to identify race based on images of people.

Race and ethnicity data can be challenging to capture, Escobar said, because of the difference between actual and perceived race and ethnicity. A new law in California, the Racial and Identity Profiling Act (RIPA), requires law enforcement officers to report the perceived race of people who have certain types of contact with law enforcement.[15] Perceived race and ethnicity are important, said Escobar, because any bias or advantage associated with a defendant's perceived race follows them throughout the criminal justice system. Ideally, data on both actual and perceived race and ethnicity would be collected to study issues like bias and disparities. Steven Raphael added that the RIPA law requires officers to check boxes for any racial identity they perceive for the defendant, and there is concern that officers might undermine the system by checking every box. Another challenge, he said, is that perception is malleable—a defendant's officer-perceived race may change depending on many factors. Gur said that he has seen cases in which a person's recorded race and ethnicity change each time they interact with the criminal justice system; this is due to data obtained from a variety of sources that collect data differently (e.g., self-report vs. perceived). Gur agreed with Stemen that collaborating with other agencies that collect self-reported race and ethnicity data could increase data reliability. Wong concurred with the need for more reliable data and said that an effort in Multnomah County, Oregon to reconcile race records among the jail, court, and prosecutor systems found that 19 percent of all cases had mismatched data on race. Another challenge with self-reported race and ethnicity data, said Kutateladze, is that people may not see themselves as fitting into the prescribed categories. For example, in his work on hate crimes in Miami, he found that people of Cuban descent systematically identified themselves as "not Hispanic," and wrote "Cuban" in the notes section. These people would be classified merely as "White" unless someone checked all the notes, said Kutateladze. To make sense of race and ethnicity information, it is important for those collecting and analyzing those data to understand the cultural issues in a given jurisdiction, he said.

In terms of data on race and ethnicity of victims, Escobar said that prosecutors who have contact with victims may be reluctant to ask questions about race and ethnicity. Victim advocates

---

[15] For more information, see
https://leginfo.legislature.ca.gov/faces/billNavClient.xhtml?bill_id=201520160AB953

might be a potential solution, Davison said, in that race and ethnicity information could come from self-identification through conversations between victims and advocates. As victims are at risk of becoming revictimized or committing an offence themselves, she argued that data on victims is important to collect, track, and report publicly.

BUILDING ANALYTICAL CAPACITY

Analytical capacity in prosecutors' offices can be built in a variety of ways, said Kutateladze, from partnering with external researchers to building in-house expertise. He asked panelists about the advantages and disadvantages of each model, and whether any one model is preferred. Using multiple approaches is ideal, Gur responded. "There is more work than there is time in the day and people to do it," he said, so utilizing both in-house and external workers can help to distribute the workload. Regardless of the model, he noted, it is critical to spend time and resources to improve processes and create efficiencies, to learn as much as possible from each data analysis and maximize every project's impact. In the Philadelphia prosecutor's office, researchers are jointly employed by both the office and University of Pennsylvania. This is "incredibly beneficial," said Gur, because these researchers not only have more research-specific expertise than others in the office, but they also gain perspective and insight from their day-to-day experiences in the office.

Wong agreed that a hybrid model, with both in-house and external research expertise, is the best approach. In Multnomah County's DA office, some internal staff work on daily data requests, while third-party researchers help with bigger projects. Having a neutral third party is important when evaluating the office's programs and policies, said Wong. In addition, third-party researchers have unique perspectives and expertise. Several years ago, said Wong, a local university helped conduct qualitative research on the workings of the prosecutor's office. Attorneys were more willing to hold honest conversations with the third-party researchers than they would have been if those conversations were conducted in-house, she said.

Stemen shared his experiences working with prosecutors' offices in Colorado. It was the first time his institution had done work with an entire state, he said, and both Loyola University of Chicago and the local prosecutors' offices wanted to have a research partner embedded locally. Stemen's organization partnered with Lauren Gase at the University of Denver/University of Colorado; she could travel to offices frequently and convene cross-site workgroups. For two years, coordinating work across the state offices was her full-time job. This put a "face on the work," said Stemen, and created sustainable relationships. University of Colorado continues to work with prosecutors' offices across Colorado and has applied for funding and grants to support the partnership, Stemen said.

A workshop participant, Adam Gamoran, William T. Grant Foundation, shared another benefit of partnerships between in-house and external researchers—the practitioner office will often build its internal capacity in response to the opportunity to work with the outside partner. This internal capacity growth, in turn, helps to strengthen and institutionalize the partnership. Stemen agreed that this is an important benefit and observed that, when his organization started work in Colorado, no prosecutors' offices had analysts. Once offices began partnering with external researchers, several offices hired their own analysts.

DATA ON PLEA BARGAINING

One aspect of data-driven work that has been especially challenging, said Kutateladze, is capturing information around plea bargaining and evidence. Assessing how and why charges change without accounting for the quality of evidence is difficult, he said, and researchers are often required to make assumptions. He asked panelists whether they have seen improvements in this area of data over time. "No," said Escobar—most offices continue to capture only the final plea accepted by the defendant, and previous offers are generally not captured in the case management system. Often, she said, the entire process is conducted via text messages between the defense attorney and the prosecutor, which makes capturing data extremely difficult. Similarly, prosecutor recommendations are frequently not captured in the case management system, or if they are captured, the office often does not analyze or report the data. Several potential reasons exist for the failure to collect data in these areas, Escobar said. First, the information may be material to the case, so attorneys do not want it shared or entered into the case management system. Second, the culture of prosecutors and defense attorneys is characterized by quick, transactional interactions, often using text message. Finally, said Escobar, attorneys might not understand the purpose of studying the "life of a plea." While a researcher may see value in studying how a plea changes over time, attorneys may largely focus on the final result.

Recent initiatives have been undertaken to collect data on pleas, Stemen said, but special effort is required to capture this information. For example, as Alexis King discussed earlier, the First Judicial District in Colorado is working to build an equity decision-making tool into their case management system. This tool will start by collecting information on bond setting, but the long-term goal is to collect information on pleas—the initial plea offer changes over time, and the final plea offer. Studying pleas is incredibly difficult, said Stemen. He and his colleagues asked prosecutors in Milwaukee about the feasibility of collecting plea-related information, and those prosecutors said that pleas are often negotiated in courtroom hallways, by text messages, or via other informal conversations. While an attorney may remember an initial plea offer and will record the final plea offer, continuous note taking would be needed to remember the intervening plea offers. Kutateladze recalled working in Manhattan, where notes on plea deals were kept on case jackets, but the notes were difficult to read. Ouss added that while it would be ideal to have data on every plea offer that was made, some information is better than none. Collecting just initial and final plea offers provides some information; for example, analysis could be conducted to determine how initial and final plea offers compare to a sentence given at trial, she said.

BUILDING DATA CULTURE

Given the importance of generating, analyzing, and using data about prosecutorial practice, asked Kutateladze, what can be done to build a strong data culture in prosecutors' offices? Stemen recalled earlier comments by King and Foxx about making data immediately useful for line staff. Effective methods, said Stemen, include creating workgroups and tasking them with addressing an issue using data analysis, or using data visualization to communicate ideas to other staff. Escobar agreed that involving staff in data projects from the outset is essential; for example, staff could check coded data or develop fields for data entry. Involving staff in these intricacies, she said, helps them understand how data can be used and why accurate data are important. Wong cautioned that prosecutors are far more likely to assist with data collection if the process is not overly complex. Gur concurred with these ideas, saying that it is also important for researchers to share findings with staff who facilitated data collection, so staff can clearly see how research translates back into practice.

One benefit of sharing data with attorneys, said Davison, is helping them "see the forest for the trees." Most prosecutors operate on a case-by-case basis; data give them the sociological view of what the team, as a collective, is doing. Sharing data can connect prosecutors to their work and educate the public on why such work is important, said Davison.

4

Prosecution Within Broader Criminal Justice, Political, and Community Ecosystems

Prosecutors working to reform systems and address racial and ethnic disparities cannot do this work alone, said Marlene Biener. Prosecution is a single part of a broad criminal justice system, and partnerships and collaborations with others in the system, as well as with communities, are essential. Several workshop sessions explored these collaborations, shared approaches to building community trust and improving accountability, and examined the evidence on effective approaches.

SETTING THE STAGE: CONSIDERING FAIRNESS AND EQUITY IN PROSECUTORIAL PROGRAMS AND PRACTICES

Kimberly Foxx shared how her personal experiences shaped her decision to become a prosecutor focused on fairness and equity. Foxx explained that she grew up in Chicago, surrounded by violence, but in a community filled with love, passion, righteousness, and justice. Foxx explained that she decided to become a prosecutor because she wanted to have the power of discretion—to decide who comes into the system, who leaves the system, who gets reunification services, and who does not. Part of what she wanted, she said, was the "power to say no" to the traditional approach. When she ran for office in 2016, Foxx said that the Chicago community was increasingly focused on prosecutors and their power and discretion. She ran on a platform including a holistic approach to prosecution and identified racial disparities in the criminal justice system as key areas of focus for her office.

After her election as State's Attorney, Foxx worked on several initiatives to address racial disparities. For example, Chicago was expending significant resources prosecuting and incarcerating people for low-level shoplifting, at a time when the city was grappling with its highest homicide rate in 20 years. Based on research and practices in other states, Foxx raised the threshold for felony shoplifting from $300 to $1,000. Her office also stopped prosecuting low-level marijuana cases and supported legislation to legalize marijuana in Illinois. Once marijuana was legalized, her office worked to vacate the convictions of individuals convicted for amounts that were now legal. Foxx's office also stopped prosecuting people for driving on suspended licenses if their licenses had been suspended for failure to pay tickets. Ninety-seven percent of the people arrested and prosecuted under this law were historically marginalized and low-income communities, said Foxx. Later, Illinois passed a law essentially preventing drivers' licenses from being suspended for failure to pay tickets.

As an elected leader of a diverse group of constituents, Foxx said it is her responsibility to decide where to focus limited resources. To do so, she considers where she can have the greatest impact for her entire constituency.

ENGAGING SYSTEMS-IMPACTED INDIVIDUALS

Ronald Simpson-Bey, JustLeadershipUSA (JLUSA), shared his experience of a wrongful felony conviction, which led to his becoming an advocate for criminal justice system change. Simpson-Bey was convicted of assault and attempt to commit murder in 1985 and sentenced to 30–50 years in prison. The conviction was overturned in 2009 on prosecutorial misconduct, he said, but the appeals process left him in prison for three additional years, until a court ordered that he either receive a new trial or be released. The prosecutor involved in his case had several other cases overturned due to misconduct; all these cases involved the same judge. To help prevent others from having similar experiences, Simpson-Bey became an advocate to change the dynamic between prosecutors and defendants. Prosecutors hold a great deal of power and sometimes abuse that power, he said, so he wanted to help prosecutors realize they could use their power in a more just manner.

Simpson-Bey currently works as Executive Vice President for JLUSA, a national criminal justice reform organization founded and operated by formerly incarcerated and directly impacted people. JLUSA was launched in 2014 with the goal of elevating the voices of people with lived experience in criminal justice reform spaces and availing them of the power and resources necessary to make change.

One part of JLUSA's work is the Justice Coordinating Council (JCC).[16] This project was inspired, explained Simpson-Bey, by President and Chief Executive Officer DeAnna Hoskins' novel interpretation of a quote from Shirley Chisholm. Chisholm said, "If they don't give you a seat at the table, bring a folding chair." Hoskins turned this idea on its head and said, "If they don't give you a seat at the table, build your own table." The JCC was launched in 2023 as a roundtable of directly impacted and formerly incarcerated people focused on policy-related work at the federal, state, and local levels. The JCC is the "connective tissue that demands change through creating a united purpose, a united voice, and establishing a united power," Simpson-Bey said.

Building and growing a group of connected, critical stakeholders is like building a choir, said Simpson-Bey. It is important for stakeholders to engage with people who have different opinions and different political views. The more people interact and share stories and perspectives, the more they change hearts and minds and can make real, sustainable changes in the criminal justice system, he said. Because of such interactions among diverse stakeholders, prosecutors are tackling challenging issues and developing new ways of approaching prosecution. For example, JLUSA partnered with the Association of Prosecuting Attorneys to convene a meeting that included representatives from myriad organizations.[17] The goal of this convening, said Simpson-Bey, was to help criminal justice actors interact with each other and with individuals who had lived experience with the criminal legal system. One result of the meeting was a published report called *A National Initiative to Advance Racial Equity in the Criminal Legal System* (Association of Prosecuting Attorneys, 2023). This report outlines a framework of authentic engagement aiming to advance racial equity in the criminal legal system, said Simpson-Bey. Based on this report, a guide was produced that outlined a process that could be used by prosecutors and other stakeholders to improve racial equity in their work. The guidelines in this *Advancing Racial Equity Implementation Guide* can be tailored to individual stakeholders according to their needs. Simpson-Bey noted that prosecutors operate in a "very

---

[16] For more information, see https://jlusa.org/jcc/

[17] Participants included the American Probation and Parole Association, the National Association for Pretrial Services Agencies, International Association of Chiefs of Police, the National Center for Victims of Crime, National Legal Aid and Defenders Association, the National League of Cities, the BJA, Bureau of Justice Assistance, Interstate Commission for Juveniles, National Association of Counties, the Office of Justice and Programs of the U.S. Justice Department, the National Sheriff's Association, Joyce Foundation, and the National District Attorney's Association.

risky situation"—they are elected officials and thus must navigate the political realities of their communities. Prosecutors' work tends to be closely scrutinized, he said. Through tools like the *Advancing Racial Equity Implementation Guide,* JLUSA works with prosecutors to help them navigate these circumstances, said Simpson-Bey. A workshop participant asked how working with directly impacted individuals can help prosecutors navigate the political context of their work. Simpson-Bey replied that people with lived experience can act as liaisons or bridges between criminal justice actors and the community, serving as credible messengers and valuable resources for elected officials. People with lived experience can also give prosecutors "political cover," said Simpson-Bey, because they are already connected to communities and have community support.

When criminal justice actors try to engage with people who have lived experience of the criminal legal system, said Simpson-Bey, "tokenism" is a risk. To avoid tokenism, it is critical for criminal justice actors to be intentional from the beginning, engaging people with lived experience in an authentic and meaningful way and bringing them to the decision-making table. People directly impacted by the criminal legal system have insight that other groups do not, and this insight is essential for developing processes, projects, and policies that can make a genuine impact. It is important for people with lived experience, in turn, to realize that their experiences make them subject-matter experts. Recognizing their own value and insisting that others recognize it as well can be beneficial in preventing tokenism, said Simpson-Bey. Furthermore, it is important for people with lived experiences to be involved in decision-making processes from the beginning, rather than simply being brought in at the end of the process. JLUSA is intentional about this process, he said: "We refuse to be tokenized; we refuse to be not at the table."

In response to a question from a workshop participant about how prosecutors could start engaging with directly impacted people in their communities, Simpson-Bey replied that prosecutors could first identify people with lived experience who also have experienced working to change the criminal legal system. Involvement in the criminal legal system may not be enough, he said, but individuals who have been involved in the system and have also engaged in inner reflection, attended school, learned, and/or been involved in advocacy work bring an invaluable perspective to the table. Simpson-Bey urged prosecutors to reach out to JLUSA for help finding such individuals. Communicating with individuals with lived experience can also humanize defendants and raise awareness of the issues they face. People who commit crimes have often faced trauma, said Simpson-Bey, and acknowledgment of this reality might improve outcomes.

Prosecutors are not the only actors that can collaborate and engage with individuals with lived experience, said Simpson-Bey. The broader criminal justice ecosystem includes communities, law enforcement, and other groups. Simpson-Bey gave the example of a partnership between JLUSA and One Voice United, a group of corrections officers and officials founded by Andy Potter. Potter worked as a corrections officer in Michigan for 28 years, around the same time as Simpson-Bey's 27-year incarceration. The two met several years after these experiences and created a program called Courageous Conversations, a one-on-one moderated conversation between Potter and Simpson-Bey that traveled around the country. In 2022, the two entered a formal partnership and conducted a retreat called Barriers to Bridges. The purpose of the retreat, said Simpson-Bey, was to bring corrections officers and formerly incarcerated individuals together to build commonality and dialogue. The retreat showed that people who seem to be on opposite ends of the criminal justice spectrum can work together in partnership for system reform. Prosecutors could do something similar, said Simpson-Bey—they only need to open their doors and have the conversations. Researchers can also benefit from engaging with people with lived experience, he said. Researchers sometimes have preconceived ideas about what they expect to observe; conversations with directly affected individuals can give researchers new ideas and avenues. JLUSA has been partnering with Research Triangle Institute (RTI International) for several years, Simpson-Bey noted.

Creating relationships and partnerships across groups requires patience and persistence, said Simpson-Bey. Building relationships with stakeholders starts with finding commonalities. As a relationship builds organically and authentically, said Simpson-Bey, partners can dive deeper into the issues they want to address together. Without support from both sides, solutions will be unsustainable, he said. It is important for stakeholders to work together, build trust and relationships, and change hearts and minds, said Simpson-Bey.

In closing, Simpson-Bey challenged prosecutors to engage with their communities as often as possible, perhaps by sending their assistant prosecuting attorney into churches, community centers, and other places to hold small, town hall-style meetings with community members. Prosecutors may believe that they are not welcome in these communities, said Simpson-Bey, but people want law and order in their communities. He also challenged prosecutors to spend the night in a jail or prison. Spending the night behind bars anonymously could "change their attitude a lot about how they approach this work." Ultimately, said Simpson-Bey, all humans want the same thing—a safe community where their children can grow and be happy.

DeAnna Hoskins, also of JLUSA, later built on Simpson-Bey's remarks. As Simpson-Bey described, JLUSA trains and invests in individuals directly impacted by the criminal justice system, said Hoskins. These individuals, she said, are not brought to the table only because they were formerly incarcerated, but because they are subject-matter experts.

When Simpson-Bey first came to Hoskins with the idea of partnering with the Association of Prosecuting Attorneys, she was surprised, as formerly incarcerated people do not seem like obvious partners for prosecutors. However, two things changed her mind. First, Simpson-Bey shared his story of incarceration and restorative justice. Hoskins thought to herself, "if a man who spent 27 years in prison for prosecutorial misconduct can give grace to prosecutors and sit at a table with them, who are you to walk away from that opportunity?" Second, Hoskins recognized the opportunity for directly impacted people to lead the conversation. At a meeting with stakeholders including sheriffs, victims, parole and probation officers, the U.S. Department of Justice (DOJ), and the White House, "everyone was taking notes as if it was a lecture" when the formerly incarcerated individuals discussed the harm the system causes. Everyone wants safe communities, said Hoskins, but the conversation about safety can only be held by humanizing people on all sides. To correct problems in the criminal legal system and ensure safe communities, it is important for every person to be seen as a human who has the right to be a productive member of society.

Steven Raphael asked Hoskins about engaging people with lived experience in research. Although there are students with significant experience inside the criminal justice system, a barrier exists when these students want to pursue research in the field. To access certain types of confidential data, researchers are required undergo a criminal background check; this check often rejects students with criminal backgrounds who might otherwise be invaluable project contributors. Students who would like to pursue Ph.Ds. and have careers in criminal justice research are unsure how to overcome this barrier, said Raphael. An adjudication process can often be used to clear people for access to confidential information, Hoskins replied. The state attorney general usually manages this process, she said; she encouraged people to work at the state level to develop a fair adjudication process that protects sensitive information but also allows people who are system-impacted to be involved in criminal justice system research. Relatedly, academic institutions can also require background checks and often do not hire people with lived experience in the criminal justice system, said Hoskins. These institutions generate large sums of money to study the system-impacted population but are unwilling to hire people from that population. JLUSA is working with several organizations to change these policies, she noted. While people who were formerly incarcerated are not a protected class under the law, said Hoskins, blanket restrictions on people with criminal convictions result in discrimination against African Americans and Latinos because they are arrested and convicted at higher rates. When considering whether a criminal conviction should prevent a person from being employed in a certain job, it is important to consider the nature of both the conviction and the job. Yale University recently changed its policies in this area and is creating a "support group" for other academic institutions that are willing to consider changing their policies, said Hoskins.

BUILDING COMMUNITY PARTNERSHIPS

Several speakers explored how prosecutors' offices can engage with communities, and the role of community engagement in shaping programs, policies, and practices. One session, moderated by Biener, focused on collaboration between prosecutors and other actors, highlighting model practices, challenges to collaboration, and the realities of prosecutorial work. Another session, moderated by Matthew Epperson, examined opportunities for prosecutors to build community confidence in the criminal justice system, particularly among historically marginalized communities. Speakers discussed collaborations established to advance programs and policies that aim to reduce incarceration or disparities; the definition of "community" in the context of their work; and their trust-building efforts.

"I sit before you as a survivor of violence," said Jamila Hodge, Equal Justice USA. She explained that her father received a traumatic brain injury during a robbery, which upended the lives of the entire family. As a result of this trauma, a sibling turned to drugs and ended up incarcerated; Hodge spent 12 years as a prosecutor. This story is not unique, said Hodge, and it is important for people to share the impact of the criminal justice system on their lives without shame. Currently, Hodge leads Equal Justice USA, a national nonprofit that works at the intersection of criminal justice, racial justice, and public health.

Hodge emphasized the need to diffuse the inspiring, uplifting learnings from the workshop to prosecutors' offices across the country—a work-intensive task, she said. Hodge highlighted several examples of actions prosecutors have taken to address racial equity issues, including John Choi's push to use a collaborative decision-making model for justice-involved youth (see Chapter 2). These champions are proximate to the issue and proximate to the people, she noted. When she thinks about "community," Hodge thinks about the people who are most impacted by violence; it is important for these people to be at the table, with access to power, and to be seen as experts on addressing problems in the criminal legal system, to create the safety communities want and deserve.

Amber Goodwin, Assistant District Attorney for Travis County, Texas, began her work in criminal justice as the founder of Community Justice, a nonprofit working to end gun violence. Goodwin said she began her work for the elected district attorney (DA) of Travis County, Jose Garza, who comes from the local community and has a background in nonprofit work. Working specifically on the intersection of domestic violence and gun violence, Goodwin defines "community" as those who are on the margins of society.

Community engagement often means bringing the community to the table, said Goodwin, but she suggested that a better approach might be to go to the "tables that the community has already put together." She said that she sometimes struggles with her identity as both a Black woman who is part of the community and as a prosecutor who has sworn an oath. Her goal is to serve all marginalized people, from victims to defendants.

After winning election in 2020, Dalia Racine, District Attorney for Douglas County, Georgia, served as the first woman and first woman of color in the role. In her career as a prosecutor in the county, Racine said she has seen a significant shift in the prosecution practices and philosophy within the community. Three pillars shape her work. The first is victim advocacy, which is based on her victimization as a child and her feeling of voicelessness; she said she wants to ensure that others who are victimized have a voice in the judicial process. The second pillar is innovation—her office has an obligation to innovate, she said, rather than taking the same actions repeatedly and expecting a different result. The third pillar is making decisions that create an equitable criminal justice system, both looking toward the future and retroactively.

These pillars have shaped her work in Douglas County, Racine said. As the smallest jurisdiction in which she has ever worked, she has found it necessary to speak up and advocate for community needs, and to make do with the limited resources available. Racine agreed with Hoskins that one of the best ways to dismantle disparities in the criminal justice system is to humanize people; as a society, "we have done a phenomenal job of dehumanizing" defendants. As part of this effort, said Racine, her office has invited previously incarcerated people to meet with the team, to broaden the team's perspectives about individuals involved in the criminal justice system. The public defender's office is another important collaborator, she said. Certain initiatives emerging from the prosecutor's office require cooperation from defense attorneys as well. In addition, the prosecutor's office supports the defense's budget requests for resources such as social workers. Racine noted an unexplored area of research—the impact defense attorneys have on the criminal legal system and on racial disparities, and whether opportunities exist for the defense bar to be proactive in addressing disparities.

Racine told workshop participants about a collaboration between her office and the local Chamber of Commerce. A research project had been conducted on restitution collection rates; the rates in Douglas County were "abysmal," she noted, and are reflective of national data. When a crime is committed and the victim can substantiate a direct financial impact from the crime, she explained, the defendant can be asked to pay that amount in restitution. This does not cover factors like pain and suffering, she clarified, but only specific items like a broken window or other damaged or missing items. Many people in the criminal justice system are either in poverty or close to poverty, said Racine, so they cannot afford these restitution fees. The DA's office asked the Chamber of Commerce to partner in soliciting funds from local businesses to start a Goodwill Guardian Program—victims with a substantiated loss can apply to this program for reimbursement, said Racine. Together, they have collected several thousand dollars to directly assist victims for items like eyeglasses, rent, and tires. The more technical aspect of this program, said Racine, is dealing with the writ of fieri facias (fi. fa.), a document victims can file to obtain restitution from the defendant at the termination of the defendant's sentence. While enforcing the writ of fi. fa. is an option for victims long after the termination of a defendant's sentence, the funds in the Goodwill Guardian Program satisfy the victim's need upfront. Victims do not have to wait years for restitution, said Racine, and the funds they receive may help to prevent poverty from pushing a victimized individual to commit criminal acts as a means of survival. Racine's office has also collaborated with the United Way and the Atlanta Regional

Commission. These collaborations aimed to provide the services and resources needed for defendants participating in a diversion program, to end the cycle of reoffending.

Yolo County is a medium-sized, diverse county in California's Central Valley, said Jeff Reisig, District Attorney for Yolo County. The population is almost half Hispanic/Latino; there is a large Asian population and smaller Black and Native American populations. Reisig was elected DA in 2006 and despite having already worked in the office for 10 years, he realized about 5 years into his elected position that he felt disconnected from communities of color in his district. In 2012, with the advice of community members, he formed the Multi-Cultural Community Council (MCCC), to serve as an advisory body to the DA.[18] "It is very easy for district attorneys to just sit in their office" and charge cases, said Reisig, but the MCCC ensures that the DA has a link with the community and understands community concerns and priorities. The MCCC consists of more than dozen people from a variety of backgrounds, he said, and they meet monthly to evaluate policies to pursue. Through collaboration between the MCCC, prosecutors, and law enforcement, said Reisig, "some really powerful things have been done when it comes to racial justice." Hodge noted that programs like the MCCC encourage prosecutors to develop relationships with the people they serve.

Tessa Smith, Yolo County Health and Human Services, currently serves as the chairperson of the MCCC. Her experience as a daughter, sister, mother and employee at Yolo County Health and Human Services, said Smith, informed her perspective when she was invited to join the MCCC six years ago. Her journey with the MCCC began when Reisig presented information to community members about racial disparities and his decision to decline to prosecute a large percentage of cases referred to him. "We all thought that was pretty good," said Smith, but the group immediately began asking questions: "What kind of cases did you decline to prosecute? Who is making all these arrests that are not being followed through on? Were people arrested? How long were they in jail? Long enough to lose their job? Long enough to break up a family and for children to be removed?" Not long after this meeting, Reisig introduced the group to Measures for Justice (see Chapter 3), to help focus the conversations needed to address these questions. In criminal justice, said Smith, sometimes everything is viewed through a crime-and-punishment lens. When community gets involved, however, "we know that every data point is a human being."

---

[18] For more information, see https://yoloda.org/progressive-programs/multi-cultural-community-council/

Biener observed that MCCC's structure involves authentic engagement—not "lip service" or simply a listening session. Genuine power sharing influences policy decisions. In addition, the MCCC bases its work on data; data provide a common language and help inform the pathway forward. Biener asked Reisig to describe some outcomes of the collaboration with the MCCC. The first major accomplishment, said Reisig, was partnering with Measures for Justice (see Chapter 3) to ensure data, which included stories, anecdotes, and heated conversations, were transparent, thorough, and fact checked. When he first approached Measures for Justice for help, Reisig noted, he had a small budget but offered to experiment with data transparency. Out of these conversations came the Commons dashboard, which is designed specifically to meet the needs of the community.[19] It was important to use an independent third party to compile and report data, to avoid suspicion around presenting data in a way showed the DA in a positive light, Reisig said. The data provided a shared understand of racial disparities and, in response to these data, the group developed a policy to expand diversion opportunities for African Americans who were being denied or not even considered for diversion. This change was a direct result of the collaboration with the community and Measures for Justice, Reisig said.

Smith described the policy in more detail. The diversion program is designed to treat the whole person and to prevent them from entering the criminal justice system; it involves mental health and substance disorder treatments as well as case management. Because the program involved service providers in the community, it expanded the DA's relationship with other institutions. Smith encourages diversion partners to consider how they invite people into the process. Many communities have reasons to distrust the criminal justice system, even if the system is offering a benefit. After the new policy to expand opportunities for diversion was implemented, diversion participation increased by 18 percent and has stabilized at an approximate 10 percent increase; much of this increase involves Black and Brown people in the community. Much work remains, said Smith. While the country is 3 percent Black, in some areas, 23 percent of all arrests are Black people. It is critical to keep the community informed and to invite people in by acknowledging the existence of disparities in the system.

Before moving into her current positions as Director of Prosecution Projects at Florida International University and co-manager for Prosecutorial Performance Indicators, Melba Pearson served for 16 years as a prosecutor in Miami. Pearson emphasized that "community is

---

[19] For more information, see https://yoloda.org/commons-data-transparency-portal/

not a monolith." When people talk about community engagement, they sometimes talk as if there is one message for everybody, she said. While there are messages that cut across communities—like fairness, justice, equity, and safety—different communities have different concerns. If a prosecutor is unable to speak to community concerns authentically, the prosecutor will not be able to develop the relationships necessary to inform and shape policies. Part of being authentic, said Pearson, is acknowledging that the criminal legal system causes harm and the prosecutor's office plays a role in that harm. Although the efforts may be awkward and difficult, Pearson encouraged prosecutors to speak with communities that have traditionally been marginalized. These groups may push back and may hold the prosecutor accountable for things that happened before their time, she said, but it is important to speak with people who are not automatic allies. Pearson advised newly elected prosecutors and those new to issues of racial disparities to acknowledge that the community has been waiting a long time for someone to listen, and to ask for grace as they attempt to tackle the important issues. Transparency and honesty, said Pearson, can be very powerful for creating a culture of moving forward together and collaborating to create a better community for all.

Building Trust with Communities

It is important to address issues discussed at this workshop with an interdisciplinary lens, said Caroline Nobo, Justice Collaboratory, Yale Law School. The disciplines of law, sciences, humanities, history, social psychology, public health, medicine, and more can all provide valuable perspectives on the conversations around safety and justice. Despite years of working with prosecutors, Nobo does not consider herself a prosecution expert—instead, she considers herself an expert on building vital communities, the importance of legitimate legal authority, and the best practices to build trust.

Nobo observed that most of the discussions around reducing racial disparities in the criminal justice system take place within an existing paradigm of deterrence; in other words, compliance and cooperation are compelled through fear of force and punishment. Instead of simply working within that paradigm, Nobo challenged workshop participants to acknowledge alternative ways of calibrating the criminal justice system's goals. For example, what if the goal was legitimacy in legal authority? When people feel that a legal authority is legitimate, she said, they trust that authority and are just as likely to follow the rules as they are under the deterrence model. As an added benefit, people are more likely to cooperate as witnesses and participate in other aspects of government, Nobo said. The public's confidence and trust in the criminal legal system is remaining static or diminishing, she said, so "something is not working here."

Prosecutors are not trained to building trust with communities, said Nobo, but they need the community's help to do their job well. The Justice Collaboratory at Yale Law School partners with prosecutors' offices to co-construct policies that build trust using a procedural justice framework. These policies are focused on restoring trust and recalibrating prosecutors' office goals to include transparency, fairness, and treating people with dignity and respect. In this work, said Nobo, "community" includes everyone—the accused, victims, witnesses, other stakeholders, and those within the prosecutor's office.

In discussing the diversion programs offered by the DA's office, Racine said that it can be challenging to get the community to accept diversion programs due to community distrust of the criminal justice system. The community is dubious about accepting help even if it is well intentioned, she said. Racial disparities exist amongst the participants who engage with accountability programs in Douglas County; one of Racine's data goals is to determine the source of these disparities. Meanwhile, the diversion program's participants more similarly reflect the community served. This creates an interesting dynamic that is important to explore to fully understand the basis of participant disparities for each program. Causes of disparities could include disparities in referral by the prosecutor's office or disparities in individuals accepting the offers; defense attorneys could be dissuading people from accepting; or people may just prefer probation over participating in a program that they may not understand or trust. Racine's group is anticipating these data, which will inform the difficult conversations required to address the disparity issue.

During her time working with the DOJ, Hoskins gained insight on "why Black and Brown people were not enrolling in drug diversion programs." One issue, she said, involves how the program is presented. When a defendant hears that his felony record will be expunged if he successfully completes a program, he might not want to take the chance of failing the program and returning to square one, facing the original charges. Even the most well-intentioned programs often have consequences for unsuccessful completion. For people who struggle with substance abuse, said Hoskins, relapse is very common during the recovery process, and defendants may not want to risk a relapse that would send them back to the beginning of the process. Zero tolerance programs are not consistent with research demonstrating the difficulty of getting clean, Hoskins emphasized; if the diversion program is created to address a defendant's addiction, why would the program penalize the defendant for being an addict, she asked. Hoskins shared a story about an individual who was facing two years in prison but was offered five years of community supervision instead. The individual preferred prison, saying that he would rather do his time and come out free instead of being nervous every day for five years and risk doing something wrong that would put him in prison for two years anyway. When a person is on probation or parole, she noted, the burden of proof that they have done something wrong is very low. It is important for prosecutors to engage with and understand the perspectives of people who have experience in the criminal justice system, said Hoskins. Honesty and transparency are critical when prosecutors are discussing opportunities and alternatives with impacted individuals, Hoskins said.

Engagement with Historically Marginalized Communities

This workshop has included discussion about the lack of trust and faith that marginalized communities have in the criminal justice system, said Epperson. He asked panelists to discuss ways that prosecutors can more successfully engage with these communities. When trying to accomplish a goal, replied Hodge, strategy, execution, and relationship are necessary components. Often, people excel at strategy and execution but are poor at relationships. Equal Justice USA, she said, focuses first and foremost on building relationships. Many prosecutors' offices have some form of community engagement. However, said Hodge, relationships are built through spending time together, listening, and two-way communication. When Equal Justice USA partners with others, the organization is intentional about starting the process by listening to the community and acknowledging its needs. "We can't just come in with our own agenda and tell people what to do," said Hodge, because they are not the experts. No one knows a particular community and its needs better than the people who live there, she said. Hodge added that it is important to consider what the prosecutor's office can bring to the community. When the community expresses a need, the prosecutor can use their power and influence as an elected official to advocate for the community and elevate community needs, helping the community to meet its needs through partnerships with other officials and service providers. Public safety, she said, is more than the absence of violence—it is necessary for a community to thrive.

The prosecutor's office staff can be leveraged for connections, noted Pearson. Each staff person is a member of some community, whether it is the LGBTQ+ community, the Black community, or an immigrant community. Prosecutors can act as ambassadors to their communities to help build trust and engagement. For example, prosecutors could tell other community members about the prosecutor's office's transparency dashboard and have conversations about which types of data people are interested in seeing. This makes community engagement everybody's job, said Pearson, and is another way to surface community issues and potential solutions.

Engaging Community to Address Violence

Epperson asked Goodwin to provide additional details about the diversion programming in Travis County and how that programming fits into the community violence intervention ecosystem. That ecosystem was built via collaborations between the DA's office, the broader community, and other partners, said Goodwin. Organizing and trying to stop violence is not a new idea, she said, and the Travis County community had long been working on these issues. When the plan was under development, some stakeholders wanted groups to work separately, in their own siloes. Instead, she said, her office brought everyone together through a mediated summit, so that all stakeholders could collaboratively discuss the plan. The product of this community process was a four-point plan that had community support even before it was implemented, with over 50 organizations and individuals signing onto it.

In the prosecutor's office, said Goodwin, the outcome is clear for certain gun charges. For example, a low-risk person who is in possession of a gun may have the case dismissed or receive a low-level charge. A higher-risk person who pulls the trigger will receive a more serious consequence. However, there are many people in the middle, for whom the outcome depends on factors like the prosecutor to which they are assigned or the court in which they end up in. Some people get deferred adjudication, she said, but receive minimal intervention during the deferral period. To keep people out of the criminal justice system, said Goodwin, those individuals need more than "a couple of classes that aren't specific to the work of reducing violence in our communities." The DA's office spent a year researching actions the prosecutor's office could take to reduce gun violence. They gathered ideas from people all over the country, examined research and data, and talked to community members, including formerly incarcerated individuals, about potential plans. Out of these efforts, a gun diversion program was developed that will target 30–50 individuals who are moderate to high risk. Goodwin emphasized the importance of community engagement to ensure the program was viewed as a community-driven initiative rather than a proposal from the DA's office, particularly when funding was sought.

Quality Improvement and Accountability

Prosecutors' offices use data dashboards and community advisory boards to both improve their practice and to stay accountable to their communities, said Epperson. He asked Pearson to discuss these and other tangible approaches to improvement and accountability. Prosecutorial Performance Indicators (PPI) has partnered with elected prosecutors and their data staff to analyze data and examine trends, said Pearson, but one element was missing: the community. Are collected data relevant to the community? Could other community values also be measured? PPI received funding to create a community engagement blueprint for prosecutors, to help them answer these questions and more, said Pearson. One important element of the blueprint involves listening sessions early in the engagement process. In these sessions, moderated by a neutral party, the community can voice its concerns while representatives from the prosecutor's office speak minimally. Often, during community meetings, elected officials talk *at* the community or present resources to them. Instead, in PPI's model, the prosecutor's office first listens to the community's description of its needs, preferred collaboration methods, and ideas for making changes. These meetings can elevate issues that may have been written off as personal problems rather than systemic problems, Pearson noted—when 10 or 20 people raise the same problem at a meeting, it points to a systemic issue.

The next step in engagement, said Pearson, is inviting community representatives to examine the proposed dashboard. It is important to include people from various community groups and particularly those who traditionally "don't have their hands on the levers of power." Community representatives can provide feedback on the data dashboard, including whether data are relevant to the community and presented in an understandable format. Next, the prosecutor can establish a community advisory board to discuss priority issues and explore potential solutions, to ensure that new policies are effective and do not cause harm. She gave the example of a prosecutor who wants to implement a diversion program that would cost $1,000 per person, but he suggests dropping the price to $500 to make it more accessible. An advisory board might tell the prosecutor that $500 is still too expensive and would not improve accessibility. Finally, said Pearson, the prosecutor can work with the advisory board to set up topic-specific boards, dedicated to topics like mental health or reentry into the community—issues based on the needs and interests of the entire community. Overall, the engagement blueprint can help prosecutors engage with their communities, hear from a variety of voices, and receive feedback on potential policy changes, said Pearson.

PROCEDURAL JUSTICE

Procedural justice is a set of evidence-based tools that prosecutors can use to make choices that elevate public trust without risking public safety, Nobo explained. Decades of research in multiple settings demonstrate that procedural justice can affect both the individual and organizational level (e.g., Tyler, 1988; Tyler & Wakslak, 2004). Individuals perceive a system or process as procedurally just when they are treated with dignity and respect and given voice, and when the decision maker is neutral and transparent and conveys trustworthy motives, she explained.[20]

Nobo relayed her experiences using the procedural justice framework to build trust. One project used "an acute problem diagnosis as a tool to learn a problem-solving technique." For example, an individual might identify a problem with respect in the prosecutor's office, such as when the prosecutor does not use the name of the accused. This problem can be used to help the office understand and solve the underlying issue, said Nobo. For one prosecutor's office, the team conducted internal and external surveys of perceptions of procedural justice. Data from these surveys resulted in changes in practice, such as editing template letters the office had been using for years and installing iPads in waiting rooms so that people could take surveys. Another office, said Nobo, completely redesigned its case screening process to be more transparent and replicable. One lesson learned during this process was that changes will not take hold unless internal office staff also feel respected and heard—that is, they feel a sense of procedural justice.

When surveying public satisfaction regarding their interactions with a prosecutor's office, Nobo noted the common assumption that a favorable outcome would be the strongest predictor of satisfaction. However, research demonstrates that procedural justice is a stronger predictor of

---

[20] For more information, see https://law.yale.edu/justice-collaboratory/procedural-justice

satisfaction than outcome favorability. Nobo and her colleagues asked the same questions of prosecutors and of different community members interacting with prosecutors and compared the answers. For example, they could ask prosecutors if they feel they are being transparent and could ask victims if the prosecutors were being transparent. It was impactful for prosecutors to see incidents in which their perceptions did not align with the perceptions of those interacting with them, and some prosecutors changed their practice in response to the identified shortcomings. Nobo's team also conducted qualitative research through interviews with prosecutors' office leadership. Leaders were often skeptical of the procedural justice framework's potential, said Nobo, even when they themselves approached the Justice Collaboratory. However, after seeing the results of the work, leaders often reported that the program had "jump-started" support for changing practices. Leaders also noted that they were pleasantly surprised by the number of community members desiring to engage in conversation, and that trust had increased among office staff.

Michael Rempel agreed with Nobo that perceptions of procedural fairness are important but observed that regardless of prosecutors' actions, community members may feel a sense of injustice based on negative interactions with police. He asked panelists to describe actions prosecutors could take to address negative perceptions of the police. Recognizing that these negative perceptions are a common topic raised in listening sessions, Pearson suggested that prosecutors could acknowledge past harms and clarify the prosecutorial role in the criminal justice system. Many people do not understand the various roles within the system, so a clear and kind explanation of prosecutors' roles could be helpful, Pearson said. She added that this approach also avoids attributing blame to the police chief, a fellow actor in the criminal justice system. Goodwin agreed with this approach, noting that her office held a series of meetings with various interest groups and advocates during which prosecutors explained each step of the criminal legal system and their role within the system.

EDUCATING COMMUNITIES ON ALTERNATIVES TO INCARCERATION

Aaron Mallory asked, "How can prosecutors work to educate the public on the need for programs like diversion, treatment, or trauma-informed care?" The process begins with "tackling the narrative," Hodge replied. Much data exists describing problems and disparities in the criminal justice system, but presenting data alone does not change the narrative. Instead, presenting both data and stories can help prosecutors to contextualize data in terms of the societal factors that led to the growth of incarceration. There is much focus on changing minds, but less on changing hearts, she said. Hearts are changed when people share stories and personal experiences. Prosecutors could help change hearts by sharing both data and stories illustrating a program's successes. Inevitably, said Hodge, problems will occur, and those stories will spread. To counter this messaging, "we need to tell the stories of the people who kept their jobs because of bail reform, who kept their children because they didn't go to prison, who kept their housing because they didn't have a conviction on their record."

Educating fellow prosecutors is another important goal, Goodwin added. Prosecutors who have done prosecutorial work for decades are trained to see the system and their goals in a certain way. Conversations about the role that prosecutors can play in changing the system, and about why they might want to do so, are critical. Implementing new programs can be risky, added Goodwin, especially if a program is the first of its kind. Sustainable implementation of policy and practice changes necessitates support from the prosecutor's office, the community, and other stakeholders—changes associated with one elected prosecutor are unsustainable, Goodwin said.

5
The Future of Prosecution

Over the course of the workshop, said Amanda Agan, speakers and participants discussed efforts to provide alternatives to incarceration, reduce racial and ethnic disparities, and decrease the potential collateral consequences of criminal legal contact. Turning to the future, she asked speakers and participants to consider promising practices in need of further evaluation, problems prosecutors face that need new solutions and new evidence, and ways to both address prosecutor needs and overcome methodological, infrastructure, and political challenges to find solutions. The workshop's final session featured a panel of speakers who discussed prosecution-related research, data needs, and policies, followed by a group conversation including reflections and takeaways from the workshop.

RESEARCH, DATA NEEDS, AND POLICY

Misdemeanors and Declination

Misdemeanors make up 80 percent of all criminal dockets in the United States, said Alexandra Natapoff, Harvard University. With over 13 million misdemeanor cases filed every single year, these cases are the most common way that people encounter the criminal legal system. Misdemeanors are also the "front line of inequality," she said, representing the first instance when poverty and race are criminalized—making misdemeanors both a profound challenge for the criminal legal system and an ideal opportunity for changes to that system. Declination is a powerful tool held by prosecutors—declining to file charges prevents an arrest from becoming a formal criminal case. The declination and charging decision can be viewed as the heart of the prosecutorial job, said Natapoff. Declination plays a crucial gatekeeping role. When a prosecutor decides whether to charge a case, she said, they are deciding for everyone— the courts, public defenders, judges, and jails. With around 10 million arrests a year in the United States, prosecutors are often faced with decisions about declination. Natapoff noted that while an arrest can be burdensome, violent, intrusive, and costly for an individual, the arrest itself is not the beginning of the adversarial process. Prosecutors are not an adjunct to the police but instead play a unique role in screening arrests and deciding whether to begin the adversarial process.

Unfortunately, said Natapoff, the misdemeanor declination process does not work as intended. Too often, prosecutors do not screen arrests up front but instead defer to police by filing low-level charges immediately after the arrest. The limited data that exist indicate that misdemeanor declination rates tend to be much lower than felony declination rates—as low as 5 percent in some jurisdictions—which means prosecutors are routinely converting arrests into criminal charges. However, ultimate dismissal rates for misdemeanors are relatively high—between 30–50 percent depending on jurisdiction. This means that a decision to drop a case could have been made right after the arrest, instead being deferred for weeks or months, Natapoff explained. The gap between the initial failure to screen and the ultimate dismissal is expensive. A defendant might be incarcerated for the duration of this gap, and they might lose their job, their benefits, and their immigration status. Most profoundly, she said, these individuals experience the weight and stigma of being a criminal defendant. This process is expensive for the entire criminal justice system because every player has to "gear up" each time a prosecutor files charges. It is also expensive from an equity standpoint—like many discretionary aspects of the criminal justice system, declination appears to be racially disparate. For all these reasons, said Natapoff, declination is an opportunity for "equitable efficiency."

Stronger screening of misdemeanors up front would keep people out of the criminal justice system, reduce racial disparities, and save an enormous amount of money, Natapoff said. Some prosecutors' offices are making changes in this area through strong declination policies, data collection, and training of junior prosecutors. When misdemeanor declination is done poorly, stated Natapoff, it ruins the lives of millions of people and costs the system millions of unnecessary dollars. Natapoff expressed hope that this area of prosecution would begin to receive increased attention.

The importance of declination was raised in an earlier workshop session, when a participant asked panelists to briefly identify "the least important thing" prosecutors' offices do; that is, if these offices had to drop something to assume a new responsibility, what could be dropped? Jamila Hodge responded that declination could free up prosecutors' time. Misdemeanors are "clogging the system," and research indicates that prosecuting misdemeanors is associated with worse outcomes than "doing nothing." By choosing to decline some misdemeanor cases, prosecutors could have more time to focus on serious crimes and issues that matter to the community, while simultaneously feeling less overworked and burned out.

Methodological and Evidence Gaps

Several speakers spoke about data or methodological gaps in prosecution-related research. Steven Raphael said that while he thinks the research community knows how to analyze data and test for causal effects, there are areas for further inquiry. For example, speakers have noted emphasized the previously mentioned lack of information on plea bargaining and noted that this information could be collected at numerous points (e.g., first offer, final offer, intermediate offer). Even obtaining data about the first offer would provide a great deal of insight, he stated. Data are also needed to describe how prosecutor decisions impact, or are impacted by, other actions at different stages in the criminal justice system. For example, Raphael said, it would be interesting to study whether cases involving use of force have differing rates of declination than other offenses.

Other interesting questions could be answered if more linkages existed between data from prosecutors' offices and other parts of the criminal justice system, Raphael noted. He described a recent project in which he learned that the California Department of Corrections uses data from the prosecutor's office, along with the defendant's sentence, to estimate an expected release date. Finally, said Raphael, more research is needed on the various promising programs that have been implemented. While many of these programs are small, it is important for programs that appear to be effective to undergo sufficiently powered research studies, in various settings and institutional contexts.

Adding his thoughts on data gaps where more research is needed, Ojmarrh Mitchell said that politicization of prosecution has eroded community trust in prosecutors and in the wider criminal justice system. He asked whether communities are aware that data dashboards exist, and whether dashboards impact community trust. He voiced that additional research is needed in these areas to restore trust in prosecutors and the criminal justice system. Patrick Robinson, VSV Leadership, agreed with the importance of performing research to explore who uses dashboards and for what purpose.

To accurately study racial disparities, said Mitchell, data describing key decision points throughout the system, from initial filing to final disposition, are necessary. A systematic literature review found many studies examining case outcomes but few that followed a case from beginning to end (Spohn et al., 2024a). The few studies that do examine the entire process often contain information from only one jurisdiction, or they contain information from multiple jurisdictions that operate under different laws. This makes it difficult to make comparisons "between different types of prosecutors operating under one unified set of state laws." The inability to compare practices can lead to a lack of accountability when prosecutors' decisions do not comport with public opinion, Mitchell said.

Mitchell shared an example from his research that illustrates the importance of data on key decision points (Mitchell et al., 2022). He and his colleagues hand-coded 12,000 records from Florida, scoring cases based on various aspects of the offense and the defendant's criminal history. One defendant, for example, scored 56 points; in Florida, this score dictates a sentence of 13.5 months in prison. This defendant, however, received a sentence of three days in jail because of a plea bargain. "Everybody pleads guilty," he said, so this type of outcome is possible for everyone. This is prosecutorial discretion in action, said Mitchell, and it is important to monitor and study its workings. This could be accomplished through a funded statewide system requiring prosecutors' offices to regularly submit data on case characteristics, case outcomes, defendant characteristics, court actors involved in the case, and other information. Mitchell noted that police and courts currently submit such data through various systems.

In terms of data infrastructure, prosecutors' offices would benefit from a list of the variables in the data system, Raphael said. He has never worked with an office that has a codebook, he observed. Another data challenge, said Raphael, is that case management systems often process raw data in ways that make data useful for managing cases but less useful for researchers. Small changes in these areas could make research considerably easier, Raphael stated.

Role of Artificial Intelligence

Patrick Robinson works as a consultant to prosecutors' offices and other stakeholders on exploring problems that can be solved with artificial intelligence (AI). The pace of AI development is accelerating rapidly, and AI use is likely to amplify and accelerate the pace at which prosecutors do their work—so it is critical to examine the underlying systems and how acceleration might lead to more inequitable results.

In considering the appropriate role of AI in the criminal justice system, Robinson said, it is important to learn from other sectors and borrow relevant models. Tools used in complex sectors ranging from physics to sales could be useful in criminal justice. For example, the healthcare sector has technology that uses algorithms to place information in the appropriate spot in the database based on a staff member's verbal description of a case. Robinson cautioned that no one recipe or formula exists for successful implementation of AI, but with resilience, curiosity, and open-mindedness, progress can be made. More research on unintended consequences of policies is important, he said, to enable actors to ask the right questions as new AI policies are being developed.

Productivity-enhancing tools currently under development could speed up many prosecutorial functions, said Robinson. He cautioned that new opportunities for some stakeholders could change the behavior of other stakeholders. Furthermore, it is important to evaluate the potential impact of AI and other new technologies on existing racial disparities or other challenges, and to monitor adoption rates and to prevent widespread unintended consequences.

John Chisholm, District Attorney for Milwaukee County, agreed that new technologies may have unintended consequences on the criminal justice system. He noted that an overwhelming amount of information is available from sources including body-worn cameras, civilian video footage, security camera footage, and recorded statements, which can add delays. It is critical to consider both the intended and unintended impacts of new technologies on the system, he said.

While some legitimate concerns exist about certain uses of AI, Mitchell argued, new tools also provide new opportunities. For example, AI can code, clean, and analyze data and run reports to monitor how prosecutors make decisions that impact racial disparities (e.g., the use of criminal history). AI can also monitor and assist with meeting internal benchmarks on case processing times. AI can be valuable for office management and overseeing day-to-day operations, said Mitchell. Another potential use of AI, said Raphael, involves natural language processing programs that can read court comments and create data that might not have been previously available.

Public Health Framework

The policies and programs discussed at this workshop, said Chisholm, involve imposing a public health framework on the criminal justice system. One way of looking at the criminal justice system is as an "accountability system for frozen moments in time," said Chisholm. Specifically, a person engages in behavior that violates the social compact, and the system attempts to prove the person did this behavior and to hold them accountable in an appropriate way, he explained. Public health systems work differently—they look at individual events to monitor the community, he said. For example, if a person comes into a clinic with a communicable disease, the main concern will be whether that disease is spreading to other community members. Over the last 20 years, there has been increasing awareness of the benefits to prosecutors from viewing themselves as part of a community public health ecosystem, he said. The American Bar Association standards for prosecutors provide the moral imperative to adopt such practices, namely in two mandates. First, prosecutors are mandated to evaluate and implement diversion practices. Second, prosecutors are more than just case processors; they are obliged to engage with their communities and help solve problems.

Chisholm opined on what it would entail if prosecutors existed in a true public health model. The district attorney's (DA) office would be actively engaged in prevention work, using data obtained from research partners to implement effective interventions at scale and in various contexts. Prosecutors would resort less to suppression models, which Chisholm said are still the predominant form of response in the criminal justice system. Approximately half of prosecutors' office staff would be working in criminal justice facilities like courthouses, while the rest would be colocated with people engaged in making their communities healthier and safer. Prosecutors would know when to take action and when to do nothing. Chisholm referred to what he called "Cool Hand Luke studies," which demonstrate the value of doing nothing in certain circumstances. An element of bluffing may exist in these situations, he noted; doing nothing may require prosecutors to appear to be doing something. Forward-thinking prosecutors are needed to address the issue of violence, Chisholm added. There is a compelling need for both research and effective policy implementation to reduce violence in communities. Violence, said Chisholm, is "the one thing that drives more bad policy than anything else."

A previous National Academies of Sciences, Engineering, and Medicine report, *The Growth of Incarceration in the United States* (National Research Council, 2014), presented four principles aiming to reduce the footprint of incarceration; these were in the areas of proportionality, parsimony, citizenship, and social justice. Prosecutors could take a similar approach, Chisholm said, creating principles to guide the practice of prosecution in a public health model. For example, one principle could stipulate that prosecutors develop and implement policies that are informed by data. Many years ago, said Chisholm, a system was envisioned that would include data about an individual's interactions with the public health system, the school system, the mental health system, and the criminal justice system. These data would be de-identified and shared for research. Much progress has been made on this system, he said, and it will eventually provide a more effective way to study why people are coming into the criminal justice system and how to address their circumstances. Such a system could be used not only to make decisions about defendants but also to offer support and resources to victims, many of whom are facing issues similar to those of defendants.

Prosecutors who implement reforms are taking political risks, said Chisholm. They attract the attention of those who prefer the system remain as it is; prosecutors are actively attacked by governors, legislatures, and dark money groups. "That's one of the risks you take," he said, noting that the risk is worthwhile to "do the right thing."

Moving Forward

Agan asked panelists to reflect on the critical questions that will confront the prosecution space in the next ten years. She listed previously identified areas for further research, including reducing the collateral consequences of incarceration, reducing racial and ethnic disparities, and improving prosecutors' capacity to build bridges to their communities. Mitchell said that future questions for prosecutors are the same questions they have been struggling with for decades— excess punitiveness, racial disparities, and inconsistent decision making. These challenges are not going away, he said, and in fact may be more difficult to deal with because of the recent politicization of prosecution.

Moving forward, Chisholm said, it will be important for prosecutors to redesign their offices. As an example, he shared the creation of the victim advocate position in the 1970s, as an attempt to increase accountability to the community. Now, he said, every DA's office in the country has a fairly robust victim advocacy department. Going forward, offices can create dedicated infrastructure for research and data collection to inform policy. Furthermore, it will be important for offices to gather more input from the community, voluntarily collaborate with partners, and cede some decision-making authority, he said. Prosecutors are tasked to act in the community's best interest, said Chisholm, with a mind toward identifying people who pose a genuine risk to the community versus those who do not.

The adversarial model of criminal justice is not a particularly flexible one, said Natapoff. To move forward and make changes, creative problem solving will be critical. Change can happen in underappreciated spaces in the criminal justice system; for example, misdemeanor declinations could change the way millions of people are treated. This approach is predicated on transparency, accountability, and public health; in contrast, the adversarial system is weighted toward confidentiality and secrecy. Changing the system will require thinking differently and having new conversations about how to achieve public safety, she said.

Agan noted that most research on reform models and policies is concentrated in big cities, and primarily in places with progressive prosecutors. She asked how research can be performed in smaller communities and communities with different perspectives on the system. One approach for broadening research, said Mitchell, could be a statewide data system to which prosecutors are mandated to report data. While a mandated system would be ideal, Raphael added, the current situation could be improved if the same case management system were used universally, so that researchers could compare and combine data across jurisdictions. Natapoff replied that the criminal justice system is designed to be "profoundly local." There are thousands of police departments, courts, and prosecutors' offices in the country; it is unlikely that a centralized data system could ever exist, she argued. While she is not opposed to a centralized data system, such a system would require overhauling the structure of a 300-year-old institution. However, she said, even conversations about transparency and research are themselves a form of progress.

While countrywide variation and discrepancy in the criminal justice system exist, said Robinson, variation can be a powerful tool for improvement because it allows for evaluation and selection of effective approaches. While this process takes time, it moves the criminal justice system in the right direction.

Earlier in the workshop, Kimberly Foxx offered her perspective on the future of prosecution. She urged constituents, researchers, academics, and other stakeholders to speak out about fairness, equity, and inclusiveness, and to insist that prosecutors be held to high standards.

Foxx noted that the medical profession is highly regulated because doctors have the potential to do harm; prosecutors can also do harm through depriving people of their life or liberty. Like physicians, she said, it is important for prosecutors to be held to high standards—including the requirement that their work be grounded in evidence and fairness.

Foxx closed by urging future prosecutors to be "brave" as they work to address unacceptable disparities in the criminal justice system. "When you are brave, you give space for other people to be brave," said Foxx.

FINAL REFLECTIONS

To close out the workshop, participants and speakers offered their final reflections and thoughts on moving forward.

Pushing the Work Forward

Workshop speakers and participants are already interested in ensuring that the practice of prosecution achieves fairness, equity, and equality, said Preeti Chauhan. However, of the thousands of prosecutors' offices across the country, many are not undertaking this work because they lack the resources, data, or funding. Structural barriers including a lack of data, inability to share data, or a lack of the legal authority to share data can limit prosecutors' offices' ability to partner with researchers, Agan added. Many offices have expressed interest in working with researchers to measure and improve the criminal justice system, she said, but doing so involves identifying existing barriers and developing solutions.

Researchers can play an important role in incentivizing prosecutors to implement evidence-based policies and practices by providing data demonstrating the cost-benefit analysis and effectiveness of practices like declination, Chauhan said. Robust messaging can also help translate research findings so prosecutors can see that declination saves money and increases public safety. Regardless of the evidence, however, prosecutors assume political risk when implementing such changes, said Chauhan.

In the criminal justice world, considerable progress has been made on data availability, access, and quality, said Brian D. Johnson. Twenty years ago, he said, no one had access to such data, and people were not even talking about using data to inform best practices in prosecution. Johnson said he is encouraged by the broad national interest in implementing evidence-based practices. There is increasing momentum behind the idea that prosecutors can use their power and discretion to impact both individual lives and the criminal justice system, said Johnson. Although effective programs have been identified, moving this work forward will involve scaling up these programs and translating them into new contexts, Marlene Biener said. Furthermore, an examination of sustainability is warranted. While "champions" may work to implement and grow these programs, ensuring that the programs outlive their creators is critical, said Biener.

Opportunities for Further Research

Workshop speakers and participants identified several areas with further research opportunities. For example, said Chauhan, diversion is a promising area for reducing both racial disparities and incarceration. However, as discussed earlier in the workshop (see Chapter 2), some research has found that Black and Brown people are less likely to participate in diversion programs, thus exacerbating disparities, she noted. Additional research could uncover why diversion is not an attractive alternative for some populations, and whether other policies such as declination may be more effective. Research is also needed on the generalizability of early, small programs and the various contexts in which policies might (or might not) work, she said.

Despite significant recent progress, the evidence base for best practices in prosecution is still "pretty thin," said Johnson. Additional research will necessitate enthusiastic funders willing to put money into this area, he said. Funding will create more research to build an evidence base from which smart, informed decisions can be made; and a stronger evidence base will attract new stakeholders. High-quality, replicable studies that examine multiple diverse jurisdictions and study outcomes over time are critically needed, said Johnson. It is important that outcomes include not just recidivism but also quality-of-life measures such as employment, education, or housing. Biener agreed with the need for additional outcome measures, noting that recidivism is an important measure—but not the only one. Additional longitudinal research could uncover alternative outcomes that may take time to observe, Besiki Kutateladze added. Adam Gamoran noted that collecting alternative outcomes could be made easier by building data linkages between the criminal justice system and other systems (e.g., education). Racial disparities are a persistent problem, he added, and concerted efforts are needed to implement programs and study their impact on disparities. In addition, research on implementation and ways to incentivize more prosecutors' offices to implement such programs is necessary, said Chauhan. Gamoran agreed, noting that data availability is not sufficient for driving change—research examining strategies for moving evidence into evidence-based practice is critical for that purpose.

Johnson also noted at the importance of investigating alternative ways of collecting data. For example, administrative data cannot be used to study defendants' perceptions of procedural justice. One interesting area for research that would require qualitative data collection, said Johnson, would be an exploration of why most defendants plead guilty.

Quoting Foxx's earlier statement, Agan said, "You cannot fix what you cannot measure." There are multiple ways of defining success—whether low recidivism, procedural justice, or racial equity—but no matter how success is defined, it must be measured to be addressed, she said.

Translation of Research Findings

One takeaway from the workshop, said Chauhan, was the importance of research-practice partnerships for generating evidence and translating it into practice. It is important for prosecutors working with researchers to be prepared to both see the data and commit to taking action to address it, she said. Partnerships between researchers and prosecutors barely existed a few years ago, Johnson noted, and now there are dozens of examples of collaborations aiming to advance a fairer, more effective system. The benefits of research-practice partnerships go both ways, he noted. Prosecutors provide researchers with context and clarity about terms, which results in improved understanding of data, and researchers provide prosecutors with feedback and actionable information about policies and practices. Some researchers, said Johnson, become disillusioned by their lack of impact; studies are often conducted and published but few people read them and the research may not be implemented. Research-practice partnerships can address this challenge, he said. Kutateladze noted that city colleges and historically Black colleges and universities could be important research partners for prosecutors' offices. Chauhan agreed, noting that many students at John Jay College of Criminal Justice have been directly impacted by the criminal justice system; there is value in researchers who have this perspective.

While further research is necessary, Biener pointed out that the current evidence base can be put into action. For example, existing evidence shows that declinations can be a powerful tool for reducing incarceration and racial disparities while protecting public safety. The challenge, she said, is disseminating this research to the approximately 3,000 prosecutors' offices across the country. A workshop participant agreed that while data gaps exist, research and implementation are an iterative process and can be started immediately. The information and passion needed to solve these complex issues already exist, he said, allowing immediate engagement in the iterative processes of development, implementation, evaluation, and redesign. While some evidence in the criminal justice field is ready for implementation, Matthew Epperson noted, not all evidence is at that point. Multiple forms of evidence exist at various stages, he said, and further research is warranted in many areas. For example, process studies could examine implementation, and qualitative studies could examine experiences of participants in programs that offer alternatives to incarceration.

Working Across the System

It is important for prosecutors' office staff to think beyond the office, toward interactions with other actors in the system. Decisions made by police shape the cases that reach a prosecutor's office, and decisions by judges critically impact outcomes for both individuals and the criminal justice system. One key takeaway from the workshop, said Biener, is the importance of building trust among the various actors in the criminal justice system, particularly the community. Procedural justice is an area of particular interest, and opportunities exist to delve more deeply into how processes can impact outcomes. Workshop participants discussed programs that include authentic community engagement and power sharing, said Biener. The workshop also highlighted victims as actors in the criminal justice system who deserve attention. The criminal justice system traditionally views victims as separate from defendants, said Biener, but panelists spoke about the commonalities between the two groups and the heightened risk for victims to become defendants. A central theme of this discussion was the importance of humanizing all actors in the criminal justice system, from victims to defendants to attorneys. Prosecutors make consequential decisions daily, Biener said, and it is important to address burnout and the overall internal climate of the prosecutor's office. If prosecutors are expected to perform their basic job functions *and* engage with the community, partner with researchers, and change their practices, it is critical that they feel supported and valued in their work.

The prosecutorial space is rapidly changing, said Epperson. Prosecutors are rethinking their role in the criminal justice system and their place in the community. It is important for prosecutors to acknowledge both what they can do and what they cannot do, and to relinquish responsibilities or share power in areas that are better suited for other actors. The public health model—which several speakers suggested could be a model for the criminal justice system—is an integrated model with multiple specialized entities working together. A move toward this model would enable prosecutors and other actors to work within and across their roles to impact inequities and disparities and begin to address root causes, said Epperson. Whether in research, policy development, implementation, or evaluation, Agan said, it is critical to include people who have been impacted by the criminal justice system.

In closing, Gamoran recalled an earlier conversation about research-practice partnerships, noting that the workshop clarified for him that the partnerships actually needed are research-practice-community partnerships. It is essential, he said, to bring the community into partnerships to build trust, to fashion a research agenda that truly captures the interests of all parties, and to develop programs that are feasible to implement. Social science researchers sometimes view their job as writing up their findings and "throwing it over the wall" for someone else to catch and run with, he said. However, "it turns out there's nobody waiting on the other side of the wall." Research rests on the relationships between the producers and consumers of research and the intermediaries who bring them together, he said. High-quality evidence is critical, said Gamoran, but it is insufficient for moving research into practice—"it's not about dissemination, it's about engagement." Solving the problems identified during the workshop, said Gamoran, "will be easier if we have a partnership with all parties aiming in the same direction."

References

Agan, A., Doleac, J. L., & Harvey, A. (2023). Misdemeanor prosecution. *The Quarterly Journal of Economics, 138*(3), 1453–1505. https://doi.org/10.1093/qje/qjad005

Association of Prosecuting Attorneys. (2023). *Building the Table: Advancing Race Equity in the Criminal Legal System.* https://www.apainc.org/wp-content/uploads/2023/02/Advancing-Race-Equity-Report.pdf

Augustine, E., Lacoe, J., Raphael, S., & Skog, A. (2022). The impact of felony diversion in San Francisco. *Journal of Policy Analysis and Management, 41*(3), 683–709.

Cossyleon, J., Orwat, J., George, C., Stemen, D., & Key, W. (2017). Deferring felony prosecution: A process evaluation of an innovative Cook County State's Attorney's Office program. *Journal of Criminological Research, Policy, and Practice, 3*(4), 261–273.

Engen, R. L., Gainey, R. R., Crutchfield, R. D., & Weis, J. G. (2003). Discretion and disparity under sentencing guidelines: The role of departures and structured sentencing alternatives. *Criminology, 41*(1), 99–130.

Epperson, M. W., Garthe, R. C., Lee, H., & Hawken, A. (2024). An examination of recidivism outcomes for a novel prosecutor-led gun diversion program. *Journal of Criminal Justice, 92*(102196).

Epperson, M. W., Sawh, L., Patel, S., Pettus, C., & Grier, A. (2023). Examining case dismissal outcomes in prosecutor-led diversion programs. *Criminal Justice Policy Review, 34*(3), 236–260.

Graef, L., Mayson, S. G., Ouss, A., & Stevenson, M. T. (2024). Systematic failure to appear in court. *University of Pennsylvania Law Review, 172*(1). https://doi.org/10.58112/uplr.172-1.1

Harrington, E., & Shaffer, H. (2022). Brokers of bias in the criminal justice system: Do prosecutors compound or attenuate racial disparities inherited from arrest? https://drive.google.com/file/d/1pPihEe_7hcIDKfFWsMGZjg91gZ9joF7E/view

Johnson, B. D., King, R. D., & Spohn, C. (2016). Sociolegal approaches to the study of guilty pleas and prosecution. *Annual Review of Law and Social Science, 12*(1), 479–495.

Johnson, B. D., & DiPietro, S. M. (2012). The power of diversion: Intermediate sanctions and sentencing disparity under presumptive guidelines. *Criminology, 50*(3), 811–850.

Kurlychek, M. C., & Johnson, B. D. (2019). Cumulative disadvantage in the American criminal justice system. *Annual Review of Criminology*, *2*(1), 291–319.

Kutateladze, B. L., Andiloro, N. R., Johnson, B. D., & Spohn, C. C. (2014). Cumulative disadvantage: Examining racial and ethnic disparity in prosecution and sentencing. *Criminology*, *52*(3), 514–551.

Mitchell, O., Mora, D. O., Sticco, T. L., & Boggess, L. N. (2022). Are progressive chief prosecutors effective in reducing prison use and cumulative racial/ethnic disadvantage? Evidence from Florida. *Criminology & Public Policy*, *21*, 535–565.

Mitchell, O., & Petersen, N. (2024). The rise of progressive prosecutors in the United States: Politics, prospects, and perils. *Annual Review of Criminology*, *8*.

National Academies of Sciences, Engineering, and Medicine. (2023). *Reducing racial inequality in crime and justice: Science, practice, and policy.* The National Academies Press. https://doi.org/10.17226/26705

National Research Council. (2014). *The growth of incarceration in the United States: Exploring causes and consequences.* The National Academies Press. https://doi.org/10.17226/18613

Nicosia, N., MacDonald, J. M., & Pacula, R. L. (2017). Does mandatory diversion to drug treatment eliminate racial disparities in the incarceration of drug offenders? An examination of California's Proposition 36. *Journal of Quantitative Criminology*, *33*, 179–205.

Ouss, A., & Stevenson, M. (2023). Does cash bail deter misconduct? *American Economic Journal: Applied Economics, 15*(3): 150–182. https://doi.org/10.1257/app.20210349

Pettus, C. (2023). Trauma and prospects for reentry. *Annual Review of Criminology, 6*, 423–446.

Prosecutorial Performance Indicators. (2022). *Reject or dismiss? A prosecutor's dilemma. A research report by the Prosecutorial Performance Indicators (PPIs) about prosecutorial case screening and dismissal practices.* https://prosecutorialperformanceindicators.org/wp-content/uploads/2022/07/PPI-Reject-Dismiss-Final.pdf

Rempel, M., Labriola, M., Hunt, P., Davis, R. C., Reich, W. A., & Cherney, S. (2018). NIJ's multisite evaluation of prosecutor-led diversion programs: Strategies, impacts, and cost-effectiveness. Center for Court Innovation. https://www.ojp.gov/pdffiles1/nij/grants/251665.pdf

Shaffer, H. (2023). Prosecutors, race, and the criminal pipeline. *The University of Chicago Law Review, 90*, 1889.

Sharif-Kazemi, H., Epperson, M. W., & Lee, H. (2021). *Principles of prosecutor-led gun diversion programming: The national landscape and current trends.* Smart Decarceration Project at the University of Chicago. https://cpb-us-w2.wpmucdn.com/voices.uchicago.edu/dist/2/1015/files/2017/01/SDP-PLGDP-Brief-Fall-2021-FINAL.pdf

Shem-Tov, Y., Raphael, S., & Skog, A. (2024). Can restorative justice conferencing reduce recidivism? Evidence from the Make-it-Right Program. *Econometrica, 92*(1), 61–78.

Spohn, C., Mitchell, O., Oramas Mora, D., & Moreira De Andrade, T. (2024b). *The effects of race and ethnicity on capital and non-capital sentencing: A systematic review and meta-analysis.* [Paper presentation]. Annual Meetings of the American Society of Criminology, San Francisco, CA, United States.

Spohn, C., Mitchell, O., White, M. D., Fine, A., & Montes, A. (2024a). *Racial and ethnic disparities in the justice system: A study of existing evidence and public policy interventions.* [Presentation]. Disparities in the Justice System Advisory Board, Phoenix, AZ, United States.

Tripodi, S., Curley, E., & Ross, S. (n.d.). *Traumatic experiences before incarceration in a county jail.* Institute for Justice Research and Development, Florida State University. https://ijrd.csw.fsu.edu/sites/g/files/upcbnu1766/files/Publications/Traumatic_exp_before_in car_county_jail.pdf

Tyler, T. R. (1988). What is procedural justice? Criteria used by citizens to assess the fairness of legal procedures. *Law & Society Review, 22*(1), 103–136.

Tyler, T. R., & Wakslak, C. J. (2004). Profiling and police legitimacy: Procedural justice, attributions of motive, and acceptance of police authority. *Criminology, 42*: 253–282. https://doi.org/10.1111/j.1745-9125.2004.tb00520.x

A

Planning Committee and Speaker Biosketches

PLANNING COMMITTEE BIOSKETCHES

PREETI CHAUHAN (she/her/hers) is a professor in the psychology department at John Jay College of Criminal Justice, City University of New York. She is also co-founder and the former director of the Data Collaborative for Justice (DCJ). Chauhan has a broad interest in examining the role of policies and practices that may create and sustain racial/ethnic disparities in the criminal legal system. Her work at DCJ has informed criminal justice policies and reform initiatives in New York City, New York State, and in other jurisdictions around the country. Chauhan currently serves on the editorial boards for Law and Human Behavior, Psychology, Public Policy, and the Law, Psychology of Violence and Journal of Community Psychology. She also serves on the Board of Directors for the New York City Criminal Justice Agency and is a member of the Council on Criminal Justice. Chauhan received her Ph.D. in clinical psychology from the University of Virginia and her B.A. and B.S. from the University of Florida. Her predoctoral clinical internship was completed at the New York-Presbyterian Hospital, Weill Cornell Medical Center. Chauhan previously served as part of a cohort for the Local Solutions Support Center, where she served as a thought partner and was paid to write a blog on prosecutorial preemption. She also wrote a piece for the Local Power and Politics Review on the same topic, in collaboration with a prosecutor, grounded in the literature. Chauhan was a member of the National Academies of Sciences, Engineering, and Medicine's Committee on Law and Justice from 2018–2023.

AMANDA AGAN (she/her/hers) is an associate professor of economics at Rutgers University. Her research lies at the intersections of economics, law, and public policy and focuses on analyzing the impact of various criminal legal policies on outcomes for defendants and on how criminal records affect employment opportunities. Agan has worked and is working with several prosecutor's offices to collect data and study the impacts of different prosecutorial and criminal legal policies. She is a faculty research fellow at the National Bureau of Economic Research and an affiliate of the Abdul Latif Jameel Poverty Action Lab - North America. Agan currently holds a grant from Arnold Ventures focused on causal impacts of prosecutorial decision making in New York and Los Angeles. She received her Ph.D. in economics from the University of Chicago.

MARLENE BIENER (she/her/hers) serves as general counsel at the Association of Prosecuting Attorneys (APA). She works directly with prosecutors across the country on criminal justice policies. Biener develops APA position statements as well as communicates with state and federal lawmakers about policy related to prosecutors and criminal justice. She oversees and designs trainings, resource guides, and APA publications to convey timely materials and education to prosecutors nationwide. Biener leads APA's work in several areas, including domestic violence, prosecutor-led diversion, procedural justice, prosecutorial data dashboards and performance indicators, and advancing racial equity in the criminal justice system. Previously, she worked for the New Jersey Office of the Attorney General, where she represented the New Jersey Division of Child Protection and Permanency. Prior to becoming a Deputy Attorney General, Biener served as a law clerk for the Honorable Wayne J. Forrest, J.S.C. She graduated from Seton Hall University School of Law. Biener is admitted to practice law in the states of New York and New Jersey, the District of Columbia, and before the Supreme Court of the United States. She attended Ramapo College of New Jersey, where she received her B.A. degree in political science, with a minor in public policy.

MATTHEW EPPERSON (he/him/his) is an associate professor at the University of Chicago Crown Family School of Social Work, Policy, and Practice, where he also serves as Director of the Smart Decarceration Project. His research centers on developing, implementing, and evaluating interventions to reduce disparities in the criminal legal system. Epperson's primary areas of focus include addressing risk factors for criminal legal involvement among persons with mental illnesses, as well as advancing evidence-based approaches to effective and sustainable decarceration. Most recently, he has led a series of multisite studies examining the effectiveness and impact of prosecutor-led diversion programs. Epperson has more than 15 years of clinical and administrative social work experience in behavioral health and criminal justice settings. He has led research studies funded by the National Institutes of Health, National Institute of Justice, the Laura and John Arnold Foundation, and the Joyce Foundation, among others. He is national Co-Leader of the Promote Smart Decarceration network, through the Grand Challenges for Social Work Initiative. Epperson led a research project on prosecutor-led gun diversion programs, funded by the Joyce Foundation, that ended August 2024. This funding was received through an invited application process. He received a B.S. in Sociology/Criminal Justice from Central Michigan, a M.S.W. from Grand Valley State University, and a Ph.D. from the Columbia University School of Social Work.

BRIAN D. JOHNSON (he/him/his) is professor and associate chair of criminology and criminal justice at the University of Maryland. His research examines court actor decision-making, inequalities in the criminal legal system, and contextual variations in prosecution and punishment. Johnson's work has been funded by organizations such as the National Science Foundation, National Institute of Justice, and Arnold Ventures. Johnson has served in key advisory roles for organizations like Measures for Justice and Prosecutorial Performance Indicators. He is a fellow of the American Society of Criminology (ASC) and is the recipient of the ASC Gene Carte Student Award, Ruth Shonle Cavan Young Scholar Award, and the DCS Distinguished New Scholar and Distinguished Scholar Awards. He is a recent co-editor of the journal *Criminology* and currently serves on the Maryland State Commission on Criminal Sentencing Policy. Johnson's published research appears in journals such as the *American Journal of Sociology*, *Criminology*, *Journal of Quantitative Criminology*, *Social Forces*, *Justice Quarterly*, and *Journal of Research in Crime and Delinquency*. He currently holds a grant from Arnold Ventures to study racial justice in prosecution in three jurisdictions in Maryland. It was obtained through a competitive grant process. Johnson received his M.A. and Ph.D. in crime, law, and justice from the Pennsylvania State University.

BESIKI LUKA KUTATELADZE (he/him/his) is a professor criminology and criminal justice at the Steven J. Green School of International and Public Affairs at Florida International University (FIU). He is also a founder and co-manager of Prosecutorial Performance Indicators, a national research and technical assistance project focusing on prosecutorial reform. Prior to his appointment at Florida International University, Kutateladze was the founding research director at the Institute for State and Local Governance of the City University of New York and before that, research director for the Prosecution and Racial Justice Program of the Vera Institute of Justice. He specializes in performance indicators, prosecutorial discretion, racial disparities, and hate crime reporting and prosecution. The FIU Provost previously named Kutateladze FIU's Top Scholar for Research, and he received a prestigious FIU Award for Excellence in Research and Creative Activity. He has served as a principal investigator on multiple National Institute of Justice-funded projects. Kutateladze received a M.A. in criminal justice from the John Jay College of Criminal Justice, a Ph.D. from the Kutaisi State University in the Republic of Georgia, and a Ph.D. in criminal justice from the Graduate Center of the City University of New York.

SPEAKER BIOSKETCHES

JOHN CHISHOLM is the (he/him/his) district attorney of Milwaukee County, Wisconsin. He has 25 years of prosecutorial experience and spent much of his early time as a line prosecutor trying to reduce gun related violent crime in Milwaukee. For example, Chisholm established and led a dedicated Firearms Enforcement Unit to address high rates of firearm related death and injury and collaborated with the Medical College of Wisconsin's Firearm Injury Research Center to identify preventative strategies to reduce harm. He believes strongly in the obligation of the elected prosecutor to engage in community-led problem solving and expanded his nationally recognized Community Prosecution Unit to place experienced prosecutors in challenged neighborhoods to partner with law enforcement and citizens to develop long term solutions to the issues of concentrated disadvantage. Recognizing the pervasive role of trauma in shaping behaviors that lead to criminal involvement, Chisholm developed an early intervention program to accountably divert people from the criminal system and worked with advocates and medical professionals to develop the Sojourner Family Peace Center, a national model that combines shelter, therapeutic intervention and collocated services for families impacted by violence. He believes strongly in partnering with academic and philanthropic institutions committed to helping justice systems better understand and address the complex challenges of racial and economic inequity in major urban centers, factors that heavily influence rates of violence.

JOHN CHOI (he/him/his) is the Ramsey County Attorney. He has become a state and national leader in progressive reform, working with public officials and impacted communities to reimagine justice and the role of prosecutors. Choi's innovative approach to working collaboratively with system and community partners has transformed the way government responds to challenges in his community. He recognizes that achieving public safety and justice for all requires continual evaluation and improvement. Providing data not only helps leaders better understand, to make better informed decisions, but also publicly increases transparency and accountability with our community, which is key to systemic transformation.

ANN DAVISON (she/her/hers) is the first female city attorney and first mom to hold the highest legal office in Seattle city government. Her career in public service began more than 30 years ago when she was a caseworker in the U.S. House of Representatives. Over the past three decades, Davison has been a champion for those without voice or power. She is committed to working with the region's criminal justice community to reduce crime in Seattle and enforce the City's laws and values. Prior to becoming city attorney, Davison worked in private practice. She has focused on areas including civil litigation, immigration, sports, contracts, business transactions, employment, and intellectual property. Davison received a B.A. in sociology from Baylor University and a J.D. from Willamette University College of Law. Afterward, she worked for the Seattle SuperSonics and was a law clerk in Marion County District Attorney's Office in Salem, Oregon, then she became a practicing attorney and arbitrator in Seattle.

GIPSY ESCOBAR (she/her/hers) throughout her career has worked in the private, public, academia, and nonprofit sectors; all of which have taught her many important lessons she applies to her work in Product today. As Measure for Justice's (MFJ's) VP of Product and Design, she's responsible for understanding the data needs of criminal justice agencies around three areas: quality, transparency, and community engagement. Escobar works cross-functionally with engineers, researchers, designers, and engagement specialists to translate these needs into solutions that improve the quality and use of data routinely collected by the system. She also provides subject-matter expertise as a criminologist and researcher to ensure that the solutions MFJ develops are responsive to the complex needs of criminal justice stakeholders and follow best data practices. As MFJ's director of research and analytics, Escobar incubated MFJ's Research Team, and worked with national experts to design and validate a system of performance measurement for local criminal justice, and to develop a robust methodology to standardize the management of criminal justice data from varied sources across jurisdictions in the United States. She holds a Ph.D. in criminal justice from the City University of New York Graduate Center and John Jay College.

KIMBERLY M. FOXX (she/her/hers) the pioneering leader of the Cook County State's Attorney's Office, as the first Black woman in this role, securing reelection. Her vision centers on transforming the office into a fairer, more transparent, and community-focused entity. Under Foxx's tenure, substantial criminal justice reforms have been implemented to enhance public safety and equity. Notable achievements include the overhaul of the Conviction Integrity Unit, resulting in almost 250 overturned convictions and a historic mass exoneration. She was instrumental in crafting the 2020 Cannabis Regulation and Tax Act, expunging over 15,000 cannabis convictions, rectifying the harms of the war on drugs, especially for communities of color. Recognizing the inequities of cash bail, Foxx spearheaded bond reform, advocating for recognizance bonds and raising the threshold for prosecution. Misdemeanor traffic offenses for unpaid fines are no longer prosecuted, allowing resources to be channeled toward addressing rising violent crime. Her commitment to transparency is demonstrated through the creation of an open data portal, providing public access to felony case-level data—a pioneering initiative nationally. Foxx is a prominent national speaker on social justice issues and has contributed to anthologies discussing criminal justice reform. Her extensive legal career includes serving as an assistant state's attorney for 12 years and advocating for children in the child welfare system as guardian ad litem. As chief of staff for the Cook County Board President, she championed racial disparities in the criminal and juvenile justice systems. Foxx is a trailblazing advocate for justice reform, transparency, and equitable public safety in Cook County. Raised in Chicago's Cabrini Green, she holds a B.A. in political science from Southern Illinois University and a J.D. from the SIU School of Law.

AMBER GOODWIN (she/her/hers) is an assistant district attorney in Travis County, Texas and founder of Community Justice. Community Justice is a gun violence prevention organization that builds power with and for Black and brown communities to end gun violence. While previously serving as executive director and currently as a senior advisor, Goodwin's leadership worked in support of over $1.9 billion in state and local funds for community focused violence intervention programs across the country. While she was executive director, the Community Justice Advocacy Fund's federal advocacy work resulted in an executive action that changed 26 federal grants across 5 agencies, worth $12 billion of federal funds to prioritize community focused violence intervention programs. She was part of the Biden-Harris Transition team as the lead organizer for gun violence prevention groups. As an assistant district attorney, Goodwin primarily works in the Special Victims Unit and serves as the district attorney's liaison to the Office of Violence Prevention for the City of Austin. She also helped in the efforts for Travis County to draw down federal funds for local community violence intervention (CVI) work, including supporting the Safer Travis County Resolution that secured one million ARPA dollars for CVI strategies like hospital-based violence prevention work and a prosecutor-led gun diversion program in 2022. Goodwin also served as chair of the Austin Gun Violence Task force which helped to create and fund 1.4 million dollars towards the city's first Office of Gun Violence Prevention in 2020. She has spent the past 25 years working for advocacy, grassroots, and electoral campaigns. Prior to founding Community Justice, Goodwin served as the first national advocacy director for Giffords, the gun violence prevention organization founded by former Congresswoman Gabrielle Giffords and United States Senator Mark Kelly.

OREN M. GUR (he/him/his) joined the Philadelphia District Attorney's Office (DAO) as director of research and a policy advisor to district attorney Larry Krasner, and now directs the District Attorney's Transparency Analytics (DATA) Lab. The DATA Lab is a new unit dedicated to using data, research, and advocacy to inform policies and practices; increase equity, transparency, and accountability; and reduce harms through prosecutorial and systems reform in Philadelphia and beyond. The DATA Lab maintains the DAO public data dashboard. His work has included prosecutor-led bail reform, decriminalizing the possession of buprenorphine and fentanyl test strips, the 100 Shooting Review, and the 57+ Blocks Coalition, and he has facilitated research on topics including bail reform, accidental drug overdoses and criminal justice contacts, the resentencing of juvenile lifers, and failure to appear among non-defendants. Gur's training is in ethnographic interviewing and neurocriminology, and his research focuses on substance use, interpersonal violence, and the application of technologies in criminal legal systems. Prior to joining the DAO, he was an assistant professor of criminal justice at Penn State Abington. Gur's B.A. in urban studies and M.S. in criminology are from the University of Pennsylvania and his Ph.D. in criminology, law & justice is from the University of Illinois-Chicago.

JAMILA HODGE (Jami) (she/her/hers) became Equal Justice USA's (EJUSA's) second leader, bringing more than 15 years of criminal justice experience as a prosecutor, policy advisor, and technical assistance provider. Under her leadership EJUSA has expanded its reach throughout the country to replace policing, mass incarceration, and executions as responses to violence with responses that advance racial equity, center those most impacted by violence, and promote safety, healing, and accountability that repairs. Hodge comes to EJUSA after launching the Reshaping Prosecution Program at the Vera Institute of Justice, where she and her team worked with progressive prosecutors, community-based organizations, and people impacted by the system to develop policy and practice reforms to end mass incarceration and reduce racial disparities within the system. One of the signature initiatives she launched was Motion for Justice, which centers racial equity in transforming the role of the prosecutor and aims to implement concrete racial equity strategies in partnership with community-based organizations. Before Vera, Hodge logged many achievements across a 12-year career in the U.S. Department of Justice as an assistant U.S. attorney for the District of Columbia. She spent four of those years as a community prosecutor focused on intervention and prevention of harm. Hodge also served in the Office of Legal Policy, where she helped shape policies for people returning from incarceration and those seeking access to counsel in criminal proceedings. Later, she worked in the office of then-Vice President Joe Biden as an advisor on criminal justice and drug policies. She has demonstrated her expertise on CBS, MSNBC, ABC Nightline, and many other media outlets. Hodge earned a B.A. in psychology and sociology at the University of Michigan and a J.D. from Duke University School of Law.

DEANNA R. HOSKINS (she/her/hers) is president and chief executive officer (CEO) of JustLeadershipUSA (JLUSA). Dedicated to cutting the U.S. correctional population in #halfby2030, JLUSA empowers people most affected by the criminal justice system to drive reform. Hoskins is a nationally recognized leader and a formerly incarcerated person with experience as an advocate and policy expert at the local, state, and federal level. Prior to joining JLUSA as its president and CEO, she served as a senior policy advisor at the U.S. Department of Justice, managing the Second Chance Act portfolio and serving as deputy director of the Federal Inter-Agency Reentry Council. Before that, Hoskins served as a county director of Reentry in her home state of Ohio. She has always worked alongside advocates who have been impacted by incarceration and knows that setting bold goals and investing in the leadership of directly impacted people is a necessary component of impactful, values-driven reform.

ALEXIS KING (she/her/hers) is the district attorney for Colorado's First Judicial District, serving Gilpin and Jefferson counties. Prior to her current role, she worked as a deputy district attorney for ten years, focusing on how children are treated in our community and leading the Human Trafficking Unit. Thereafter, King served as a magistrate judge in Denver and worked as a Title IX and victim rights attorney at the Rocky Mountain Victim Law Center. Since taking office, she has created a Conviction Integrity Unit, enforced bond reform, developed a prefile diversion program, and led Colorado in the largest prosecutorial data transparency project in the country. King earned a B.A. at Hollins University in Virginia and graduated from the Sturm College of Law at the University of Denver.

AARON MALLORY (he/him/his) is the founder and chief executive officer of GRO Community. He founded GRO Community to assist males, particularly males of color, that are often misunderstood and outcasted within our society. Mallory has more than 10 years in the field, working with specifically African American males with diverse behavior challenges. He has provided direct service work at UCAN within their transitional living shelter for young adult males, HRDI as a child and adolescent therapist. Mallory has served in leadership roles as the clinical supervisor at HRDI and clinical director at Heartland Alliance Readi initiative.

OJMARRH MITCHELL (he/him/his) is a professor in the Department of Criminology, Law & Society at the University of California, Irvine. His research focuses on criminal justice policy, particularly in drug control, sentencing, corrections, and racial fairness within the criminal justice system. More broadly, Mitchell examines the effectiveness and equity of criminal justice sanctions. His recent work investigates prosecutorial discretion and its impact on case processing, outcomes, and racial disparities in Florida's courts. Mitchell has received several awards for his research on racial and ethnic issues in the criminal justice system, including the Western Society of Criminology's W.E.B. Du Bois Award and both of the National Institute of Justice's W.E.B. Du Bois Awards. He has served in numerous advisory roles, such as on the U.S. Department of Justice's Science Advisory Board, New York City's Pretrial Research Advisory Council, Philadelphia's Pretrial Reform Advisory Council, and the Executive Board of the American Society of Criminology. Mitchell is also the vice president-elect of the American Society of Criminology and the editor-in-chief of *Criminology & Public Policy*.

ALEXANDRA NATAPOFF (she/her/hers) is an award-winning legal scholar and criminal justice expert; she is the Lee S. Kreindler Professor of Law at Harvard Law School. She writes about criminal courts, public defense, plea bargaining, wrongful convictions, and race and inequality in the criminal system. Her book *Punishment Without Crime: How Our Massive Misdemeanor System Traps the Innocent and Makes America More Unequal* (Basic Books) reveals the powerful influence that misdemeanors exert over the U.S. criminal system. Natapoff's book *Snitching: Criminal Informants and the Erosion of American Justice* (NYU Press), won the American Bar Association Silver Gavel Award Honorable Mention for Books. Her original work on criminal informants has made her an international expert. Natapoff is a Guggenheim fellow, a member of the American Law Institute, and a graduate of Yale University and Stanford Law School. She has helped draft state and federal legislation, and her work appears frequently in judicial opinions as well as the national media. Prior to joining the legal academy, Natapoff served as an assistant federal public defender in Baltimore, Maryland.

CAROLINE NOBO (she/her/hers) is a research scholar in law and executive director of the Justice Collaboratory at Yale Law School, where she provides strategic direction and leadership to the Justice Collaboratory's unique network of interdisciplinary scholars and staff.

Her research as a criminologist focuses on promoting trust and legitimacy in the criminal legal system. Nobo's expertise includes procedural justice, policing, gun violence, data systems, community-based research methodologies, and the progressive prosecutor movement. She is the co-author of the book *Legitimacy-Based Policing and the Promotion of Community Vitality*. She is often featured translating research into policy for global audiences, and lectures at universities across the world. Nobo sits on the board for a Connecticut non-profit serving incarcerated parents and their children. Prior to joining Yale, she was the director of data outreach for the non-profit Measures for Justice, and a senior researcher at Abt Associates. She holds a B.A. in sociology from Mount Holyoke College and a M.S. in criminology from the University of Pennsylvania.

AURÉLIE OUSS (she/her/hers) is an assistant professor in the Department of Criminology at the University of Pennsylvania. Her research examines how good design of criminal justice institutions and policies can make law enforcement fairer and more efficient. Ouss' work, conducted in collaboration with court actors in place like New York, Philadelphia or Paris, has been published in journals such as *Science, The Journal of Political Economy*, or *The Quarterly Journal of Economics*. She has been leading a team of researchers at the University of Pennsylvania embedded at the Philadelphia District Attorney's Office, which has facilitated increasingly impactful and nuanced analyses of the justice system. Ouss received a B.A. in econometrics and sociology from École Normale Supérieure, a Master's in economics from the Paris School of Economics, and a Ph.D. in economics from Harvard University. She had a postdoctoral fellowship at the University of Chicago Crime Lab.

MELBA PEARSON (she/her/hers) is an attorney specializing in civil rights and criminal law, with an emphasis on policy. She is the director of prosecution projects at the Gordon Institute for Public Policy, and co-manager for the Prosecutorial Performance Indicators (PPI) project based at Florida International University. The PPIs aim to bring more transparency, equity, and racial justice to the criminal justice system. Pearson also serves as faculty in the Department of Criminology and Criminal Justice. She has a consulting practice through her firm MVP Law, which includes victims' rights work, assessments of police departments and creating community engagement strategies around criminal justice/civil rights issues. Before joining FIU,

Pearson spent three years as deputy director of the American Civil Liberties Union of Florida. She worked to change police practices, expand voting rights, and reform the criminal justice system. Previously, Pearson was an assistant state attorney in Miami-Dade County for 16 years, culminating as assistant chief in the Career Criminal/Robbery Unit supervising junior attorneys while prosecuting homicides. She serves as chair-elect of the American Bar Association Criminal Justice Section, and immediate past president of the National Black Prosecutors Association Foundation. Pearson regularly provides legal analysis for CourtTV, Law & Crime, local networks, and through op-eds that have been published in the Miami Herald, Washington Post, and other national outlets. She is the editor/author of the book *Can They Do That? Understanding Prosecutorial Discretion*. Lastly, she hosts a video podcast show #MondayswithMelba, as the Resident Legal Diva. Pearson was the progressive candidate for Miami Dade state attorney, garnering a strong showing across party lines.

CARRIE PETTUS (she/her/hers) is a leading social work scholar dedicated to advancing social equity and wellbeing among those involved in criminal legal and justice systems. As the founder and chief executive officer of Wellbeing & Equity Innovations, she collaborates with government and community partners to improve outcomes through research-practitioner partnerships. Pettus' research expertise includes trauma, behavioral health, violence, and family systems in criminal legal and justice settings, such as diversion and deflection, incarceration, and reentry. Her work is recognized for its impact on the field. Pettus has been widely published, is a frequent speaker at conferences and other events, and her research has been featured in major media outlets. Committed to data justice, she chairs the Grand Challenges for Social Work, focusing on addressing social inequities. Pettus' research has significantly influenced policies and practices, establishing her as a key figure in using research to drive systemic change. With a Ph.D. from the University of North Carolina at Chapel Hill School of Social Work, Pettus has also served as a faculty member at Washington University in St. Louis and Florida State University.

HAROLD F. PRYOR (he/him/his) was elected Broward state attorney (Florida's 17th Judicial Circuit). He leads a staff of 462 employees, including 213 prosecutors, whose mission is to make our community safer while working to ensure justice, equity and fairness for everyone affected by our criminal justice system. Pryor is the first Black state attorney in Broward and the first Black man to be elected state attorney in Florida. His legal career includes experience as a prosecutor, a civil attorney in private practice, and as a corporate lawyer. Pryor started his legal career serving as a Broward assistant state attorney prosecuting serious criminal offenses. He also practiced in the private sector where he specialized in business litigation, the Federal Communications Commission, consumer-related issues, employment law, and commercial transactions.

DALIA RACINE (she/her/hers) is the Douglas County district attorney. She was elected as the first woman and person of color to serve in this role in her community. Racine brings almost 20 years of prosecutorial experience where she specialized in crimes against women and children, human trafficking, and homicides. She has championed the role of prosecutors to keep communities safe by implementing innovative practices that reduce potential repeat offenders who cause harm by connecting them to resources that bring individual and community healing, while also holding dangerous offenders accountable in our prison system. Racine serves on numerous boards across Metro Atlanta that impact community change.

STEVEN RAPHAEL (he/him/his) is professor of public policy and the faculty director of the Institute for Research on Labor and Employment at University of California, Berkeley (UC Berkeley). He holds the James D. Marver Chair at the Goldman School of Public Policy. Raphael's research focuses on the economics of low-wage labor markets, housing, and the economics of crime and criminal justice policy. His is a research fellow at the National Bureau of Economic Research; the California Policy Lab; the University of Chicago Crime Lab; IZA, Bonn, Germany; and the Public Policy Institute of California. Raphael holds a Ph.D. in economics from UC Berkeley.

JEFF REISIG (he/him/his) has been a prosecutor for over 27 years and has been the Yolo County's chief elected law enforcement official. During his tenure as district attorney, he has focused intently on advocating for victims of crime and pursuing a balanced approach to public safety through methods designed to enhance accountability while also embracing programs to reduce recidivism and the criminal justice footprint.

MICHAEL REMPEL (he/him/his) is director of the Data Collaborative for Justice at John Jay College of Criminal Justice, a research center that focuses on mass incarceration, racial and ethnic disparities, and low-level enforcement. His current work includes overseeing a multiyear study of New York's bail reform law; analyzing New York City's jail population and identifying promising strategies to reduce it; and studying racial disparities at multiple stages of the criminal justice continuum. Rempel previously worked at the Center for Court Innovation, serving as the agency's founding director of jail reform and, before that, serving for 16 years as the agency's research director. In the final years of his tenure, he was the lead-author of a data-driven roadmap for reducing New York City's use of incarceration; led multiple studies related to risk-need assessment; studied racial disparities in misdemeanor arrests and prosecutions; and co-created and evaluated a pilot project to reduce court backlogs in Brooklyn, New York. In the first decade of the 2000s, Rempel led numerous studies examining drug treatment courts, diversion programs, and court responses to intimate partner violence.

PATRICK ROBINSON (he/him/his) is the founder and owner of VSV Leadership, a consultancy specializing in organizational leadership, coaching, project management, design thinking, and data/management opportunities. He co-founded Prosecution Leaders of Now, a national leadership development community for prosecutors featuring coursework hosted by the Stanford University Graduate School of Business. Prior to starting VSV Leadership, Robinson led strategy and grant-making for innovation in prosecution at the Chan Zuckerberg Initiative. He is an experienced military prosecutor and former special assistant U.S. attorney in the Western District of Texas. During his service in the U.S. Army, Robinson served as a prosecutor and defense counsel, and he deployed to Afghanistan during Operation Enduring Freedom as a Special Operations legal advisor. Following his military service, he returned to school as a Pat Tillman Scholar, earning a M.B.A. from Stanford University and graduating as an Arjay Miller Scholar. Patrick received a law degree from the University of Virginia, and he received a Bachelor's degree from the University of Notre Dame.

MONA SAHAF (she/her/hers) is the director of Vera's Reshaping Prosecution initiative, which helps communities increase public safety by shrinking the front end of the legal system, addressing racial disparities in prosecution, and increasing prosecutors' collaboration with the people most impacted by their decisions. Before joining Vera in 2021, she worked as a federal prosecutor in the Human Rights and Special Prosecutions section at the U.S. Department of Justice (DOJ) and in the U.S. Attorney's Office for the District of Columbia, focusing on domestic violence and national security cases. At DOJ, Sahaf built a program to protect Central American migrants who were kidnapped in Mexico. In addition to her work at Vera, she serves on the boards of organizations working to preserve Kashmiri culture and secure human rights in Kashmir. Sahaf holds a B.A. in history and government from Georgetown University and a J.D. from Boston University School of Law.

HANNAH SHAFFER is an assistant professor at Harvard Law School. Her research uses empirical methods to study how discretion moves through the criminal legal system—from arrest to charging to sentencing to rearrest—and how decision-makers' beliefs impact their discretionary choices. Shaffer recent research uses administrative court records to examine racial disparities in criminal charging and sentencing—specifically how prosecutors interpret and respond to racial disparities inherited from police and earlier decision-makers in the criminal process. To understand more holistically what drives these empirical patterns, she surveys prosecutors and links their reported beliefs to their real-world decisions. In future work, she plans to explore how racial disparities in individual police officers' arrests impact downstream charging and sentencing decisions. Shaffer has several scholarly works that are recently published or under revision, including "Prosecutors, Race, and the Criminal Pipeline," 90 U. Chi. L. Rev. 1889 (2023); "Brokers of Bias: Do Prosecutors Compound or Attenuate Racial Disparities Inherited at Arrest?" with Emma Harrington; and "Prediction Errors, Incarceration, and Violent Crime," with Emma Harrington and William Murdock III. She received a B.A. from Washington University in St. Louis, J.D. at Harvard Law School, and a Ph.D. in economics at Harvard University.

RONALD D. SIMPSON-BEY (he/him/his) is a national leader in the movement to decarcerate America, currently working as the executive vice president of Strategic Partnerships for JustLeadershipUSA. He is also an alumnus of their Leading with Conviction Fellowship. Simpson-Bey is an LPI Trained Leadership Coach and is prominently featured in the book, *Halfway Home: Race, Punishment, and the Afterlife of Mass Incarceration* by Reuben Jonathan Miller. He is also a contributing author to the book, *Smart Decarceration: Achieving Criminal Justice Transformation in the 21st Century*. Simpson-Bey serves as the vice-chair for the American Bar Association (ABA) Criminal Justice Section Victims Committee, and as a special advisor for the ABA Criminal Justice Section council. He serves on the Advisory Committee for the Prison and Jail Innovation Lab at the Texas LBJ School of Law. Simpson-Bey also serves as the board president of the Michigan Center for Youth Justice, as the board treasurer for the National Legal Aid & Defender Association, as a co-founder of Nation Outside in Michigan, and is a co-founder of the Michigan Collaborative to End Mass Incarceration. Simpson-Bey attended Eastern Michigan University, Mott Community College, and Jackson Community College.

TESSA SMITH (she/her/hers) works for Yolo County Health and Human Services Agency in Woodland, California. She started her work as a family partner and community educator on mental health and suicide prevention. This work informed her involvement with the Health and Human Services Agency HSA Cultural Competence Committee for years before evolving to her current Diversity, Equity, and Inclusion Coordinator role. Smith's work includes multi-level engagement on health and racial equity issues at an interpersonal, community, and systemic level. She has been a district attorney's Multi-Cultural Community Council (MCCC) member for seven years and the MCCC chair for the past five years.

DON STEMEN (he/him/his) is a professor in the Department of Criminal Justice and Criminology and co-director of the Center for Criminal Justice at Loyola University Chicago. He was previously the director of research on sentencing and corrections at the Vera Institute of Justice. Stemen's research focuses on criminal case processing, prosecutorial decision making, and prosecutorial performance measurement, and he is currently one of the co-managers of the Prosecutorial Performance Indicators—a national effort to improve the data and analytic capacity of local prosecutors' offices. He has over 20 years of experience working with local, state, and national government partners to reform criminal justice practice and policy. Stemen's work has been supported through grants from the National Institute of Justice, the National Institute of

Corrections, the Bureau of Justice Assistance, the John D. and Catherine T. MacArthur Foundation, Arnold Ventures, the Microsoft Justice Reform Initiative, and the Open Society Foundation. He received his Ph.D. in law and society from the Institute for Law and Society at New York University.

CAROLINE WONG (she/her/hers) is a Multnomah county deputy district attorney who has prosecuted a wide variety of misdemeanor and felony offenses over the past 20 years. She currently supervises attorneys in the Child Support Enforcement Division and is assigned other duties focusing on research and evaluation, grant writing/management, specialty courts, and innovative diversion programs. Wong served as a community prosecutor for many years, working closely with community members and neighborhoods on livability issues. She was a part-time criminal justice instructor at Portland Community College and a legal instructor for the Portland Police Bureau. Wong worked as a law clerk for the Oregon Department of Justice Appellate Division and as a civilian for the Department of Defense Judge Army General (JAG) Corps in Kaiserslautern, Germany. She received a Bachelor's Degree from Pacific University and her J.D. from the University of Oregon School of Law.

B
Workshop Agenda

8:30–9:00   **Registration open and breakfast available**

9:00–9:10   **Welcome and Introduction**

Moderator: Preeti Chauhan, John Jay College of Criminal Justice, CUNY, Workshop Planning Committee Chair

9:10–9:45   **Setting the Stage: Considering Fairness and Equity in Prosecutorial Programs and Practices**

Kim Foxx, State's Attorney for Cook County

Moderator: Preeti Chauhan, John Jay College of Criminal Justice, CUNY, Workshop Planning Committee Chair

9:45–11:00   **Reducing Disparities and Alternatives to Criminal Justice Involvement: Evidence Across Prosecutorial Decision Points**

Amanda Agan, Cornell University, Workshop Planning Committee Member

Hannah Shaffer, Harvard Law School

Ojmarrh Mitchell, University of California, Irvine

Alexis King, District Attorney for Colorado's First Judicial District

Moderator: Brian Johnson, University of Maryland, Workshop Planning Committee Member

11:00–11:15   **BREAK**

11:15–12:45   **Reducing Disparities and Alternatives to Criminal Justice Involvement: Evidence from Diversion Programs**

Steven Raphael, University of California, Berkley

Michael Rempel, Data Collaborative for Justice

Matt Epperson, The University of Chicago, Workshop Planning Committee Member

Aaron Mallory, Gro Community

Moderator: Preeti Chauhan, John Jay College of Criminal Justice, CUNY, Workshop Planning Committee Chair

12:45–1:45   **LUNCH**

1:45–3:00   **Prosecutorial Perspectives: Implementing Promising Programs, Policies, and Practices**

Harold Pryor, State Attorney for Florida's 17th Judicial Circuit (*virtual*)

John Choi, District Attorney for Ramsey County (*virtual*)

Carrie Pettus, Wellbeing & Equity Innovations

Mona Sahaf, Vera Institute

Moderator: Marlene Biener, Association of Prosecuting Attorneys, Workshop Planning Committee Member

3:00–3:15   **BREAK**

3:15–4:45   **Data Use and Data Culture in Prosecutor Offices**

Don Stemen, Loyola University of Chicago

Gipsy Escobar, Measures for Justice

Oren Gur, Philadelphia's District Attorney Office

Ann Davison, City Attorney for Seattle

Caroline Wong, Deputy District Attorney for Multnomah County (*virtual*)

Moderator: Besiki Kutateladze, Florida International University, Workshop Planning Committee Member

4:45   **MEETING ADJOURNS—END OF DAY 1**

TUESDAY, SEPTEMBER 24, 2024

8:30–9:00   **Registration open and breakfast available**

9:00–9:05   **Welcome**

Moderator: Preeti Chauhan, John Jay College of Criminal Justice, CUNY, Workshop Planning Committee Chair

9:05–9:45   **Setting the Stage: Prosecution Within Broader Criminal Justice, Political, and Community Ecosystems**

Ronald Simpson-Bey, JustLeadershipUSA (*virtual*)

Moderator: Matt Epperson, University of Chicago, Workshop Planning Committee Member

9:45–11:00   **Advancing Programs and Policies Through Collaboration with Criminal Justice Actors**

Aurélie Ouss, University of Pennsylvania

DeAnna Hoskins, JustLeadershipUSA

Dalia Racine, District Attorney for Douglas County (*virtual*)

Jeff Reisig, District Attorney for Yolo County (*virtual*)

Tessa Smith, Yolo County Health and Human Services (*virtual*)

Moderator: Marlene Biener, Association of Prosecuting Attorneys, Workshop Planning Committee Member

11:00–11:15   **BREAK**

11:15–12:30   **Building Partnerships with Community**

Jamila Hodge, Equal Justice USA

Amber Goodwin, Assistant District Attorney for Travis County

Melba Pearson, Florida International University

Caroline Nobo, Yale Law School, Justice Collaboratory

Moderator: Matt Epperson, University of Chicago, Workshop Planning Committee Member

12:30–1:15   **LUNCH**

1:15–2:45   **The Future of Prosecution: Research, Data Needs, and Policy**

Alexandra Natapoff, Harvard University

Steven Raphael, University of California, Berkeley

Ojmarrh Mitchell, University of California, Irvine

Patrick Robinson, VSV Leadership

John Chisholm, District Attorney for Milwaukee County (*virtual*)

Moderator: Amanda Agan, Cornell University, Workshop Planning Committee Member

2:45–3:00   **BREAK**

3:00–4:00   **Final Reflections**

Workshop Planning Committee Members

Moderator: Preeti Chauhan, John Jay College of Criminal Justice, CUNY, Workshop Planning Committee Chair

4:00   **MEETING ADJOURNS—END OF DAY 2**